1800 QUOTES, QUIPS,
AND SQUIBS

1800 QUOTES, QUIPS, AND SQUIBS

by
E. C. McKenzie

BAKER BOOK HOUSE
Grand Rapids, Michigan

ISBN: 0-8010-5898-8

1. The proper way to greet a visiting bureaucrat is to roll out the red tape.
2. In Spain, the man who throws the bull is called a matador. In this country, we call him a senator.
3. Anyone who can walk to the welfare office can walk to work.
4. Foreign Aid is where they take money from the poor of a rich country and give it to the rich of a poor country.
5. Maybe it would be a good idea to get those protesters to lay off the war for awhile and work on death and taxes.
6. When you get to heaven you will likely see many people there you did not expect to see. Many will be surprised to see you there, too.
7. If you think you're getting too much government, just be thankful you're not getting as much as you're paying for.
8. The trouble with the world is that there are too many clowns who aren't in the circus.
9. At any moment the United States Supreme Court is expected to declare all of us unconstitutional.
10. The family that smokes together chokes together.
11. Some people will never live to be as old as they look.
12. It is a mistake to judge a man's horsepower by the size of his exhaust.
13. Nothing is as easy as it looks, except spending money.
14. Some people, even after they come in, keep on knocking.
15. When we hear some popular songs, we are sure the illiteracy rate is still pretty high.
16. If you want to be different these days, just act natural.
17. About the time a man gets his temper under control, he goes out and plays golf.
18. Some people grow up and spread cheer. Others just grow up and spread.
19. If you really would like to test your strength, why not try lifting a mortgage?
20. After-shave lotion and cologne top the gift list on Father's Day—thus proving that everybody loves dear old dad, but nobody likes the way he smells.
21. This is an age of tension. Almost everybody lives in fear of bending an IBM card.

22. Things are pretty well evened up at the present time. Other people's troubles are not as bad as yours, but their children are a lot worse.
23. Discipline is what you inflict on one end of a child to impress the other.
24. Odd as today's teen-agers appear, none of them look as awed as their parents.
25. Autumn is that magic time of year when you look out and the pool is no longer filled with your neighbors' kids. It's filled with your neighbor's leaves.
26. A farmer reported an increase in egg production immediately after posting the following sign in the hen house, "An egg a day keeps Colonel Sanders away."
27. The man who can smile when things go wrong has probably just thought of somebody he can blame it on.
28. Politics and music are much alike. The person who is off key always seems to have the loudest voice.
29. If life's best things are free, food is not one of them.
30. The world is going to the dogs. Watch how people sit up and beg.
31. A counterfeiter is the only guy who gets into trouble by following a good example.
32. Be grateful for your doors of opportunity—and for friends who oil the hinges.
33. When we have nothing as our target we usually hit it with amazing accuracy.
34. Many men consider it a good day at golf it they don't fall out of the cart.
35. You can always recognize a wise man by the smart things he does not say.
36. It's what the guests say as they pull out of the driveway that really counts.
37. The government is mainly an expensive organization to regulate evil-doers and tax those who behave.
38. A successful man is one who works hard to get rich and then spends the rest of his life sitting on the porch of a sanitarium watching the healthy poor go by.
39. The best way to keep good intentions from dying is to execute them.
40. To balance your budget, rotate your creditors.
41. Attention wives: There is very little difference in husbands. You might as well keep the first.
42. If at first you don't succeed, you'll get a lot of free advice from folks who didn't succeed either.
43. A revolving charge account can get you pretty dizzy by the tenth of every month.

44. There are always two sides to a peace conference—but no end.
45. If flattery is the food of fools, why are we so starved for it?
46. Nothing makes people more sensitive to pain than giving until it hurts.
47. The wages of sin are unreported.
48. It takes all kinds of people to make a world—and it's about time they got started.
49. Today it is difficult to tell whether some of our older youth are spoiled or just naturally smell that way.
50. Most people have presence of mind—the trouble is absence of thought.
51. Perfect mates come only in gloves and shoes.
52. As we grow older, we find the best time for a cold shower is some other time.
53. What we don't know may not hurt us, but it surely doesn't help either.
54. Bachelors have no idea what married bliss is. And that's true of a lot of married men.
55. The warmth of a home is not necessarily determined by its heating system.
56. It's better to help others get on than to try to tell others where to get off.
57. Nobody is for anything he doesn't understand.
58. Nowadays, the only time men turn the other cheek is when they get their sideburns trimmed.
59. An Oklahoma farmer recently said that everything his teen-age son ate turns to hair.
60. Eat, drink and be merry—because tomorrow they may cancel your credit card.
61. War is one thing you can't get in economy size.
62. The trouble with some people who don't have much to say is that you have to listen so long to find that out.
63. There is no better night spot than a good, clean bed. *with his own wife*
64. How often do you think of the shut-ins, the locked-ups, or the down-and-outs?
65. You can buy a load of dirt for $10.00—either for your lawn or your library.
66. We lie loudest when we lie to ourselves.
67. The world changes so fast that a man couldn't be wrong all the time if he tried.
68. Ask not for whom the telephone bell tolls; if thou art in the bathtub, it tolls for thee.
69. The penalty good men pay for neglecting politics is to be governed by their inferiors.
70. Adult education can begin with teen-age marriage.

71. The worst tragedy to befall a man is to have ulcers and still not be a success.
72. The best things in life are free; also the worst advice.
73. A hamburger by any other name costs more money.
74. Recently a poverty-stricken couple got married. They are going to practice planned parenthood. They plan to live either with her parents or his.
75. If you haven't figured out where you are going, you are lost before you start.
76. Those who think their tax dollar doesn't go very far should glance toward the moon occasionally.
77. Maybe Congress should divert some of that Foreign Aid to the post office.
78. We are only young once. That is about all society can stand.
79. The easiest way to find a cop is unexpectedly.
80. Courtesy is a form of consideration for others practiced by civilized people when they have the time.
81. World problems are now so confusing that computers are asking questions.
82. If at first you don't succeed, find someone to blame.
83. You get out of life just what you put into it—minus taxes.
84. Said a banker's son, "My pop went on a diet; there was too much collateral in his blood."
85. A Sunday golfer is a person who is more concerned with a hole-in-one than the Holy One.
86. Experience is a great teacher, but often has trouble with her pupils.
87. More and more people are saving pennies these days—they don't know what else to do with them.
88. Enthusiasm for hard work is most sincerely expressed by the person who is paying for it.
89. It is obvious that what makes some people tick needs winding.
90. The average man, poor fellow, falls for more things than he stands for.
91. If the divorce rate continues to climb, some day the marriage ceremony will change from "I do" to "perhaps."
92. The rush hour is when traffic is at a standstill.
93. If you can't grow old gracefully, do it any way you can.
94. Most all our young men start out in life expecting to find a pot of gold at the end of the rainbow. By the time they are middle-aged, most of them at least have found the pot.
95. Almost all doctors specialize today—and the specialty of some is banking.
96. Nothing can increase prices more these days than including the tax.

97. Maybe it isn't proper and right to take a defeatist position, but aren't prospects poor for abating air pollution in an election year?

98. Newspapermen sometimes risk their lives to bring home a story. Other men sometimes risk their lives with the stories they bring home.

99. If the creation of the world had been a federal project, it probably would have taken six years instead of six days.

100. Anyone who doesn't worry about the world situation these days must be getting lousy reception on his television set.

101. The mortality rate of cigarette smokers and non-smokers is 100 percent. The only difference is the timing!

102. About the only thing some people do for their town is grow old in it.

103. A thumbprint on the Bible is more important than a footprint on the moon.

104. Tension is driving with the brakes on.

105. A girl can often stop a man from making love to her by marrying him.

106. The man who steps into a cage with a dozen lions impresses everybody except a bus driver.

107. What we need in Washington are not Hot Lines but firm lines.

108. A wise man acknowledges his mistakes. A fool will defend his.

109. The man who believes he is exerting himself beyond the call of duty is apt to be a poor judge of distance.

110. It's time to think about dieting when you try to push yourself away from the table and it's the table that moves.

111. Most of the things that come to a fellow who waits are not the things he was waiting for.

112. Nothing helps a fellow to talk on his feet more than having something to say.

113. It probably would be all right if we'd love our neighbors as ourselves—but could they stand that much affection?

114. Fifty years ago a man who drove 25 miles an hour in his automobile was a sensation—and he would be today, also.

115. An efficient business man who found a machine that would do half his work at the office bought two.

116. Education helps you to earn more, but not many school teachers can prove it.

117. The person who closes his mouth before someone else wants him to has passed one of the tests of success.

118. As people get better off, they sometimes have too much to live on and too little to live for.

119. When you sing your own praise, you always get the tune too high.

120. Keep smiling, it makes everybody wonder what you're up to.
121. The happiest ending in the movies is when the guy behind you finishes his popcorn.
122. An optimist is a husband going to the marriage bureau to see if his license might have expired.
123. Sign in front of a church, "The competition is terrible but we're still open on Sundays."
124. An important young man in Texas recently joined the Navy so the world could see him.
125. No one can stay young long, but some manage to act like children all their lives.
126. Old timers remember when only rich people played golf and paid income taxes.
127. The world is better, either because you lived in it, or because you left it.
128. A few of us can still remember when the drugs of youth were sulphur and molasses.
129. In the early days many of our great men wore long hair and beards, but they didn't carry a guitar.
130. All some people do for a cold is sneeze.
131. It is said that to dress an American soldier, it takes the wool of two sheep and the hides of three taxpayers.
132. Educational TV has proved quite successful. Just having a set repaired is a good lesson in economics.
133. Yesterday's political promises are today's taxes.
134. Any bachelor knows that June rhymes with Moon, Spoon, Groom and Doom.
135. It is impossible to make wisdom hereditary.
136. A boaster and a liar are first cousins.
137. The trouble with most boards of education is that they are not used in the right place.
138. To err is human—but usually a much better excuse is demanded.
139. By its very nature music has the ability to take you away from everything that's ordinary.
140. Forgiveness is a funny thing; it warms the heart and cools the sting.
141. A diplomatic husband said to his wife, "Why do you expect me to remember your birthday when you never look any older?"
142. Old golfers never die. They just get tee'd off and putt away.
143. A broken character doesn't knit easily.
144. Taxes are staggering but they never go down.
145. Most all men used to jog when they were younger—only then they called it chasing the girls.

146. Money no longer talks—it stutters.
147. Middle-age is when men don't get any younger and women any older.
148. Intuition is what makes a woman able to contradict her husband before he says anything.
149. A banker is a guy who lends you an umbrella when the sum is shining and wants it back when it starts to rain.
150. Many of today's college students feel they can clean up the troubles of the world. One parent stated he'd be satisfied if his student-son "just cleaned up his room."
151. All good things come to the other fellow if you wait.
152. About the hardest thing to get hold of these days is easy money.
153. There are two sides to every question except when it happens to be a love triangle.
154. We may have a lot of excitement in some of our dreams but nobody ever wakes up in the morning breathless.
155. The trouble with working for the future is that you usually end up with an awfully dull past.
156. A person's faith is not judged by what he says about it, but by what he does about it.
157. No matter what the fashion is, some people are always either the wrong size, the wrong shape, or the wrong age for it.
158. What gives you away is what you give in to.
159. There is nothing original about any of our sins. They have all been tried before. None has worked.
160. Language is the apparel in which our thoughts parade before the public. Let's never clothe them in vulgar or shoddy attire.
161. A fool and his money are soon parted. The rest of us just wait until income tax paying time.
162. It is true that two can live as cheaply as one—if they both have good jobs.
163. Greatness is largely by comparison. A ship looks huge at the dock, but tiny when at sea.
164. A cocktail party is where you spear olives and stab friends.
165. Are you frustrated? If so, just remember that the great oak is a little nut that held its ground!
166. Perhaps sex education does have a place in our schools. If that won't get kids to read, nothing will.
167. Times are always hard for those who seek soft jobs.
168. Few children are guilty of thoughtless mischief. They plan it.
169. The big question today is not what the world is coming to, but WHEN.
170. A running mate is a husband who dared to talk back.

171. Faith is more than thinking something is true. Faith is thinking something is true to the extent we act on it.
172. There is nothing like horseback riding to make a person feel better off.
173. It's the itch to be rich that keeps us scratching.
174. Sign in a sportswear store, "Buy your girl a bikini—it's the least you can do for her."
175. A switch in time saves crime.
176. America—love her or leave her.
177. If at first you don't succeed, try trying.
178. Advertising helps raise the standard of living by raising the standard of longing.
179. A jaywalker is one who probably doesn't make the same mistake twice.
180. It is beginning to look like a lot of people these days are under the influence of affluence.
181. The biggest disadvantage to keeping a diary is a peeping mom.
182. Once again the cost of living is up. Next thing you know, taxes will be a bargain.
183. These days, a child who knows the value of a dollar must be mighty discouraged.
184. Any smart woman will tell you that the way to a man's heart is through his ego.
185. Worry is like a rocking chair; it gives you something to do, but it really doesn't get you very far.
186. Life is a stage and a lot goes on behind the scenes.
187. There's no end to the population explosion—the whole world's going stork mad!
188. Perhaps we should add a fifty-first star to our flag to represent the confused state of our nation.
189. Nothing adds age like reviewing an old high school annual.
190. Man is a complex being: he makes deserts bloom—and lakes die.
191. Funny how a dollar can look so big when you take it to church, and so small when you take it to the store.
192. If life expectancy keeps increasing, will we reach the age of discretion?
193. One good thing about the future is that it never lasts.
194. Some people resemble elevator operators—they never go out of their way.
195. It looks like collective bargaining is all collecting and no bargaining.
196. A table of bridge is a place where a lot comes out that is not in the cards.
197. Unless the job means more than pay, it will never pay more.
198. Children wear out teachers almost as fast as shoes.
199. Prayer helps prevent moral hibernation and spiritual anesthesia.

200. A bachelor is a man who has only his own dishes to do.
201. Nothing is so apt to cling to the family tree as the sap.
202. One hippie to another, "I always say, if the shoe fits—steal it."
203. When things go wrong, don't go with them.
204. Reputations are not always ruined. Sometimes they're confirmed.
205. Those who live happily ever after probably were not after very much.
206. There is a town in New Mexico so small it has mini-outskirts.
207. If you don't think a girl is dynamite, try dropping one.
208. Measure a man by the size of his ideas and the height of his ideals.
209. We usually see things not as they are, but as we are.
210. Each time inflation takes another bite out of the dollar, we usually get indigestion.
211. You can't feel down in the mouth with the corners up.
212. People don't really pay much attention to what we say about our religion, because they'd rather watch what we do about it.
213. If taxes go much higher a guy will have to work like a dog to live like one.
214. Luxuries are things that make people do without necessities.
215. Today's college student demonstrators seem to be marching backward into the future.
216. The wisest among us is a fool in some things.
217. With many people, this pay-as-you-go plan is at a standstill.
218. Prayer can change afflictions into affirmatives, adversities into opportunities, and burdens into blessings.
219. Some people will pat you on the back before your face and hit you in the eye behind your back.
220. The "Three R's" of citizenship include Rights, Respect and Responsibility.
221. Giving a penny for some peoples' thoughts is just another example of inflation.
222. It is beginning to look like some folks put everything they've got on their backs to try to build up their fronts.
223. The man who moved the mountain began by carrying away small pieces.
224. Maybe the reason folks can't figure out some of our public figures is because some of our public figures don't add up.
225. Anyone who breathes deeply these days probably doesn't care about his health.
226. The politician who can be bought sooner or later gives himself away.
227. A fool empties his head each time he opens his mouth.

228. The most successful man is the one who holds onto the old just as long as it's good and grabs the new just as soon as it's better.
229. To insure the education of teen-agers, parents need to pull a few wires—TV, telephone, ignition, etc.
230. "I'm stork mad," wailed the father of thirteen children.
231. The whisper of temptation is heard farther than the loudest call to duty.
232. If the going is getting easy, you're not climbing.
233. The dollar may not go as far as it used to, but what it lacks in distance it makes up in speed.
234. Close your eyes to the faults of others and watch the doors of friendship swing wide.
235. The trouble with telling a good joke is that it always reminds the other guy of a dull one.
236. A fellow who plugs into current affairs these days is liable to get a shock.
237. The emptiest man in all the world is the man who is full of himself.
238. When we go too far it's seldom in the right direction.
239. In the United States money is power and there is no substitute.
240. Difficulties need not be disastrous; defeats need not be fatal; failures need not be final.
241. A bargain is something we buy and can't explain it.
242. Hide your head in the sand and you won't leave many footprints on it.
243. More people enjoy baseball than football because it doesn't require a college education to get tickets.
244. We seldom are aware of what's cooking until it boils over.
245. Statistics can be used to support anything—including statisticians.
246. The only book that really tells you where to go on your vacation is your checkbook.
247. Your religion is of no value to you unless it makes you worth something to someone else.
248. Oversleeping will never make one's dreams come true.
249. A light foot on the gas beats two under the grass.
250. This will be a better world when the power of love replaces the love of power.
251. The true measure of a man is the height of his ideals, the breadth of his sympathy, the depths of his convictions, and the length of his patience.
252. Those who do not cross rivers until they get to them usually have fewer rivers to cross.
253. We have too many people who live without working, and we have altogether too many who work without living.

254. Most men flirt with the women they would not marry, and marry the woman who would not flirt with them.
255. Pray earnestly; you can't expect a thousand-dollar answer to a ten-cent prayer.
256. If one chooses to be a knocker, he needs neither brains nor education.
257. Sometimes it looks like a fellow has to do unto others a mighty long time before they start to do unto him.
258. If you're going around in circles, maybe you're cutting too many corners.
259. Parents can tell but never teach unless they practice what they preach.
260. You may be sure that the man who leaves his footprints on the sands of time was on his toes the biggest part of the time.
261. Beseeching will carry you further than lambasting.
262. We are sure to judge wrong if we do not feel right.
263. Then there is the barber whose specialty is road-map shaves; when he's done, your face is full of short cuts.
264. Monday is a terrible way to spend one-seventh of your life.
265. Anti-cigarette commercial, "Truth or cancerquences."
266. When life kicks you, let it kick you forward.
267. Pretty blondes are perhaps the only girls who manage to get ahead by starting at the top.
268. Movie stars make good politicians—they've got years of acting experience behind them.
269. A flimsy excuse is one that your wife can see through.
270. The most expensive thing a community can buy is a cheap educational program.
271. Knowing without doing is like plowing without sowing.
272. Did you hear about that beatnik girl who was getting married? Instead of her friends giving her a shower, they made her take one.
273. It's not those who lie awake at night that succeed, but those who stay awake days.
274. Many a genius discovers he isn't smart once he gets out of his teens.
275. Flattery will get you nowhere. Especially when you give it to yourself.
276. WHO is right is never as important as WHAT is right.
277. It does a man no good to sit up and take notice if he keeps on sitting.
278. A recent poll showed that LBJ was the best president the United States ever had. The poll was taken on the LBJ ranch.
279. If a young man becomes a road engineer, should he become known as a "roads" scholar?
280. Old hotheads never die; they just lose their cool.

281. In most neighborhoods, it is the gabbiest people who call themselves the silent majority.
282. There's no more certain way of losing face than shooting it off.
283. Attitudes and beliefs, like factories and machines, sometimes need re-tooling and overhauling.
284. Television has changed the family circle to a semi-circle.
285. Temptation is not sin but playing with temptation invites sin.
286. The only person who saves time is the one who spends it wisely.
287. It seems no matter how you encourage your children to trod the path of righteousness, they insist on following in your footsteps.
288. Our paychecks are usually like the tide—they come in and go out.
289. Advice to public speakers: Stop talking just before the audience stops listening.
290. The old-fashioned girl who used to go to the city and stop at the YWCA now has a daughter who goes to the city and stops at nothing.
291. Mother Nature fills some stockings better than Santa Claus.
292. The connecting link between the animal and vegetable kingdom is stew.
293. As kids, most of us started smoking cigarettes because we thought it was smart. Why don't we stop for the same reason?
294. A cheap but top-rate computer is the one between your ears.
295. Why is it that a person who has nothing to do always thinks he needs a busy person to help him do it?
296. Marriages may be made in heaven but their success depends on how long they stay in orbit.
297. It's not the way he kicks but the way he pulls that makes the mule valuable.
298. A fellow sure has to use his noodle these days to keep out of the soup.
299. Time is money—especially overtime.
300. All things come to him who waits—on himself.
301. The first prize for being the laziest man in the world has to go to the fellow who sits and whittles with an electric knife.
302. Sign in a service station, "Difficult days have come and lit—too tired to work, too poor to quit."
303. You can't lose weight simply by talking about it. You must keep your mouth shut.
304. It is better for most folks to be at a loss for words than at a loss for thoughts.

305. A pedestrian is a man who has two cars, a wife and a son.
306. No woman is likely ever to be elected President—they never reach the required legal age.
307. A close relative is one you see occasionally between funerals.
308. In Russia, it doesn't take a fellow long to talk his head off.
309. There is no greater satisfaction than parking on what's left of the other person's nickel.
310. A New Year's resolution is something that goes in one year and out the other.
311. About the only thing you can save out of your pay these days is the envelope.
312. Did you hear about the Scot who was building a new home, and called up the Masonic Hall to send him two free masons?
313. If you want a job done fast, give it to a busy executive. He'll have his secretary do it.
314. A supersalesman is a husband who can convince his wife she's too fat for a mink coat.
315. Socialism is not an equal distribution of wealth. It is equal distribution of poverty.
316. A little boy told his teacher there were three sexes: Male, female and insects.
317. Now when your ship comes in, the government sees that it is docked.
318. Won't it be wonderful when income taxes get back down where we can afford to make a living?
319. Television came along to prove that some radio programs are as bad as they sound.
320. Money makes unhappiness pretty comfortable.
321. Nine-tenths of the people couldn't start a conversation if the weather didn't change once in a while.
322. The reason a man's hair turns gray quicker than his whiskers is because it has a twenty-year start.
323. Honesty may be the best policy—but there are some people who don't seem to think they can afford the best.
324. If you think the world owes you a living, hustle out and collect it.
325. Etiquette is knowing which finger to put in your mouth when you whistle for the waiter.
326. All marriages are happy. It's the living together afterwards that causes all the trouble.
327. Church sign: We specialize in guidance systems.
328. The trouble with life is that by the time a fellow gets to be an old hand at the game, he starts to lose his grip.
329. Middle-age is when you've given up everything you can and still don't feel good.

330. Lots of things are more important than money. The trouble is that you need money to buy them.
331. A modern miracle would be a diamond anniversary in Hollywood.
332. Advice to girls: be an old maid and look for a husband every day or marry and look for him every night.
333. It's funny how people on a diet are never reduced to silence.
334. Adam was the only man in the world who couldn't say, "Pardon me, but haven't I seen you before?"
335. A high-pressure salesman once sold a farmer two milking machines for one cow and then took the cow as a down payment.
336. If wives knew what secretaries think of their husbands, they wouldn't worry.
337. You can be positive or negative; hopeful or cynical; joyful or miserable—take your pick.
338. If Mother Nature could have foreseen bermuda shorts, she surely would have done a better job on the male knee.
339. One good place to study ancient history is in the doctor's waiting room.
340. Conscience is that something which prompts a man to tell his wife before someone else does.
341. Cooperation would solve most problems. For instance, freckles would be a nice coat of tan if they'd get together.
342. Nobody ever made a law that will prevent a man from making a fool of himself.
343. Courtship is that period during which a girl decides whether or not she can do any better.
344. "Puppy love" is just a prelude to a dog's life.
345. Bill collectors always call at the most inopportune time— when you're at home.
346. Discretion is something a feller learns after it's too late to do him any good.
347. A doctor in Texas has made enough money so that he can occasionally tell a patient there is nothing wrong with him.
348. The most common causes of embezzlement, according to a recent survey, are slow horses and fast women.
349. An executive is a businessman who wears out several suits to every pair of shoes.
350. Except for wrestlers, no really big man ever throws his weight around.
351. Appearances are deceiving. A dollar looks the same as it did twenty years ago.
352. Matrimony is one state that permits a woman to work eighteen hours a day.

353. Anybody who thinks talk is cheap has never argued with a traffic cop.
354. In the United States today, the big farmer is the only man who can lose money every year, live well, educate his children and die rich.
355. Nothing changes the line of a man's thoughts quicker than spading up a fishing worm while digging in the garden.
356. Golf is like children. It takes time and patience to master them.
357. History must repeat itself because we weren't listening the first time.
358. The little voice inside used to be conscience. Now it's a pocket radio.
359. Just about everybody will agree that our country is on the move, however, there is considerable argument about the direction it is moving.
360. Most of the time our will power suffers from generator trouble.
361. The best way to serve the leftovers is to somebody else.
362. He who blows his stack adds to the world's pollution.
363. An automobile can help you see the world, but it's up to you to decide which world.
364. The Ten Commandments were given to man in tablet form, and by following directions could save a lot of other tablets from being used.
365. Too many of us spend our time the way politicians spend our money.
366. There's only one trouble with resisting temptation—it may never come again.
367. It's better to appear ridiculous than not appear at all.
368. The village hippie isn't totally worthless; at least, all the parents in town can cite him to their children as a horrible example.
369. The guy who screams the loudest for the right to dissent is usually the first to deny it to those who disagree with him.
370. If you want to speed a package through the mails try stamping it, "Fresh Fish."
371. Hard work won't kill a fellow if he can stay far enough away from it.
372. A hospital patient's life is bound to have some aches and pans.
373. To discourage glue-sniffing, a horseradish scent has been added to the cement used in making plastic models.
374. In the use of words, too, quality is more important than quantity.
375. The average man's ambition nowadays is to be able to afford what he is spending.

376. Courtship is the short interlude between lipstick and mop-stick.
377. About the time one makes good marks in the school of experience he is old enough to retire.
378. This country was founded partly to avoid taxation. Our founding fathers should take a look now!
379. A bachelor is a fellow with no buttons on his shirt—or on his lip.
380. How do birds know you have just polished your car?
381. A budget is an attempt to live below your yearnings.
382. The only one who watches the clock during the coffee break is the boss.
383. Nobody ever gets hurt on the corners of a "square deal."
384. There is a lot more begging done on expensive letterheads than with tin cups.
385. A theory is a hunch with a college education.
386. One of the quickest ways to meet new people is to pick up the wrong golf ball on the golf course.
387. She who wears a strapless evening gown worries not about cost, but upkeep.
388. A bigamist is a man who has taken one too many.
389. Pity poor old George Washington. He couldn't blame his troubles on the previous administration.
390. Opportunity has to knock, but it's enough for temptation to stand outside and smile.
391. A short-cut is usually the quickest way to get to where you weren't going.
392. When a child pays attention to his parents, they're probably whispering.
393. Where there is no faith in the future, there is no power in the present.
394. There's too much talk about enforcing laws and not enough said about obeying them.
395. You never get a second chance to make a good first impression.
396. In truth, inflation is something like the Hong Kong flu. It's hard to trace and hard to stop.
397. Many a man with no family tree succeeded because he branched out for himself.
398. Nowadays when a girl says her new evening gown is really nothing, she means it.
399. Lies, like chickens, come home to roost.
400. The test of tolerance comes when you are in the majority.
401. Sign in a car on a city freeway, "Attention car thieves—this car is already stolen."
402. Money is what things run into and people run out of.

403. Always put off until tomorrow what you are going to make a mess of today.
404. An organ recital is women discussing their operations.
405. A neighbor's noisy, cheap old car can be very annoying; but so can his quiet, new, expensive one.
406. Middle-age is the time of life when work begins to be a lot less fun and fun begins to be a lot more work.
407. Romance is like a game of chess—one false move and you're mated.
408. The fourth of July—that's when we celebrated our freedom in 1776 from unfair British taxation. Then, in 1777, we started our own system of unfair taxation.
409. Wise men are not always silent, but they sure know when to be.
410. Some people's idea of physical fitness consists of exercising their opinions about the actions of others.
411. A new taxpayer sent the Internal Revenue Department 25 cents with a note saying he understood that he could pay his taxes by the quarter.
412. Look at it this way—the number of divorces in America proves it's the land of the free. The number of marriages shows it's the land of the brave.
413. There are two kinds of men who never amount to anything. One cannot do what he is told, the other cannot do anything unless he is told.
414. Talk and the world talks with you. Think and you think alone.
415. A teen-ager is a youngster who is old enough to dress himself—if he could remember where he dropped his clothes.
416. Religion is not to save us from trouble, but to save us from defeat.
417. People who cough never go to the doctor. They go to the theater.
418. We may complain about the heat in the summer, but at least we don't have to shovel it.
419. Future generations won't be squandering their hard-earned money—we've already done that for them.
420. One of the first things a boy learns with a chemistry set is that he isn't likely to get another one.
421. Said the photographer to the lady, "Look pleasant, please. As soon as I snap this picture you can resume your natural expression."
422. Getting to the moon looks easier and easier as time passes. It's staying right here on earth that seems tougher and tougher.

423. It's true that everybody is entitled to the pursuit of happiness, but it looks like too many want the government to finance the chase.
424. The American businessman has a problem; if he comes up with something new, the Russians invent it six months later and the Japanese make it cheaper.
425. Federal Aid is like giving yourself a blood transfusion by drawing blood from your right arm, returning it to your left arm, and spilling more than half of it on the way across.
426. Youth looks ahead, old age looks back, and middle-age looks tired.
427. There are lots of people who believe that distant relatives are the best kind.
428. Mini-skirts may be fine and dandy. But somehow a man thinks they always look too short on his wife and daughter.
429. Your age depends on the elasticity of your spirit and the vigor of your mind—and on how many birthdays you're still looking forward to.
430. One good way to have a clear mind is to change it occasionally.
431. What many a store clerk gets for Christmas is an ulcer.
432. The easiest way to guess a woman's age is without her help.
433. You can't go in the wrong direction and arrive at the right destination.
434. A careful driver is one who just saw the driver ahead of him get a traffic ticket.
435. What the world needs is a closer agreement on what the world needs.
436. Modern prosperity means two cars in the garage, a boat in the driveway, and a note due at the bank.
437. When both the speaker and the audience are confused, the speech is "profound."
438. Too many people are ready to carry the stool when there's a piano to be moved.
439. You must give these backseat drivers credit for one thing. They never run out of gas.
440. When a husband has the last word it's apt to be in his will.
441. Men play golf religiously—every Sunday.
442. An egotist is a man who thinks as much of himself as you think of yourself.
443. Everybody likes a good loser—provided it is the other team.
444. A man owes it to himself to become successful; after that, he owes it to the Bureau of Internal Revenue.
445. Many a man works hard to keep the wolf from the door; then his daughter grows up and brings one right into the house.

446. Fish grow faster than any other living thing. In fact, the average fish that is caught grows about six inches every time the story is told.
447. Some folks think they are busy when they are only confused.
448. Courage is something you always have until you need it.
449. We do our best on saving money when we haven't got any.
450. Most automobiles keep owners pretty well strapped even without seat belts.
451. Be careful when you give advice because somebody might take it.
452. Nonchalance is the ability to look wise when you've acted foolishly.
453. Columbus took a trip on borrowed money and established the custom on our shores.
454. The smart husband never asks who is boss around the house.
455. Some folks think that traveling around in the best circles makes them big wheels.
456. The height of unimportance is that sensation you have when you make a mistake and nobody notices it.
457. One should pity the blind, but it's hard to do if the rascal is the umpire.
458. A bargain is something you cannot use at a price you cannot resist.
459. Then there was the fellow who said the only reason he was so lazy was because it kept him from getting so tired.
460. "Practice does not make a lawyer perfect," says a famous judge. But enough of it will make him rich.
461. An executive is a man who can take two hours for lunch without hindering production.
462. Baldness is man's oldest fallout problem.
463. If the grass is greener on the other side of the fence, you can bet the water bill is higher.
464. Years make all of us old and very few of us wise.
465. People who live in glass houses make very interesting neighbors.
466. A man has arrived when he can be as cranky at the office as at the breakfast table.
467. Unhappiness in marriage is due to illness—they're sick of each other.
468. Experience has been defined as "compulsory education."
469. The joys of motherhood are what a woman experiences every day—when the kids are finally in bed.
470. Retirement is the time of life when you stop lying about your age and start lying about the house.

471. The world really isn't any worse. It's just that the news coverage is so much better.
472. Good after-dinner speaker: One who pops in, pops off, and then pops out.
473. Dentists have more faith than anybody. It's a miracle that more of them don't get their fingers bitten off.
474. It's a small world until you start chasing your wind-blown hat down the street.
475. An echo is pretty accurate, but it doesn't contribute much that is new.
476. He who keeps his mind on his work, goes ahead; he who keeps his work on his mind, goes mad.
477. Lack of pep is often mistaken for patience.
478. Nowadays the world revolves on its taxes.
479. Modesty is the art of encouraging people to find out for themselves how important you are.
480. Benjamin Franklin may have discovered electricity but the man who invented the meter made all the money.
481. An open mind is fine—if it isn't accompanied by an open mouth.
482. We usually judge others by ourselves.
483. Cosmetics are beauty products used by teen-agers to make them look older sooner, and by their mothers to make them look younger longer.
484. If you think twice before you speak, you'll never get into the conversation.
485. A budget is a contraption that shows how much you are going to have to borrow.
486. The reason most people know so little about what's going on in the world is that this information isn't in the comic strips.
487. Where did you get the idea that swimming is good for the figure? Did you ever take a good look at the whale?
488. Listening to advice may get you into trouble, but it makes the other person feel better.
489. Opinion is prejudice with a few unrelated facts.
490. One woman's definition of retirement, "Twice as much husband on half as much money."
491. If you feel that you have no faults—that makes another one.
492. The awkward age is when you are too old for the Peace Corps, and too young for Social Security.
493. An adolescent is a minor who is a major problem.
494. Prosperity is that wonderful time when you can always get enough credit to live beyond your means.
495. A pessimist absorbs sunshine and radiates gloom.

496. Although unpaid bills are by no means rare, they are nevertheless considered collector's items.
497. Many parents of teen-agers seem to agree that one "hang-up" their kids don't have is when on the phone.
498. A fellow who was on welfare stood in line so long to get his handout that he asked the government to pay the parking ticket on his Cadillac.
499. Christmas holidays mean anticipation, recreation, prostration, and recuperation.
500. Husband to wife, "I'm telling you—one more TV dinner and you had better look for a new sponsor."
501. The best way to serve spinach and parsnips is to someone else.
502. Regardless of what the Supreme Court says, there will be prayers in our schools as long as there are exams.
503. Man is the only animal who goes to sleep when he isn't sleepy and gets up when he is.
504. Today's progressive American is one who wears last year's suit, drives this year's car, and lives on next year's salary.
505. If you're gonna be a sneak—at least be open and above board about it.
506. One of the troubles with small talk is that it usually comes in large doses.
507. The eyes of the community are upon you. What do they see?
508. What this country really needs today is a credit card that will fit in a vending machine.
509. You can't fool all the people all the time, but income tax forms come close.
510. A good scare is often worth more to a man than good advice.
511. It's too bad that more people are thoughtless than speechless.
512. The worst thing about retirement is having to drink coffee on your own time.
513. He who laughs last usually has an insecure upper plate.
514. The small boy who voluntarily washes behind his ears is probably looking for his chewing gum.
515. No man is a successful liar unless someone believes him.
516. The home may lose popularity, but there never will be a substitute place to eat corn-on-the-cob.
517. Too many hosts seem to think that the best way to open a conversation is with a corkscrew.
518. Poise is the ability to be ill at ease naturally.
519. When you are down and out, something always turns up— and it is usually the noses of your friends.

520. If you want to know what your wife is going to ask you to do next, try sitting down.
521. Congress is confronted with the unsolved problem of how to get the people to pay taxes they can't aford for services they really don't want.
522. Take the humbug out of this world, and you haven't much to do business with.
523. Fish seem to grow faster during the first few weeks after they are caught.
524. Prosperity is what keeps us in debt.
525. No man is so full of wisdom that he has to use his mouth as a safety valve.
526. A straw vote only shows which way the hot air blows.
527. Profanity is the effort of a feeble mind to express itself forcibly.
528. It may be a man's world, but chances are it's in his wife's name.
529. The trouble with industry is that there are too many one-ulcer men holding down two-ulcer men's jobs.
530. If the kids are running this country, we wish they'd set the grown-ups a little better example.
531. The average taxpayer is the first of America's natural resources to be exhausted.
532. If an automobile dealer drives a new car 500 miles, it is nicely broken in; if we drive it 50 miles, it is a used car.
533. To a brave man, good and bad luck are like his right and left hand. He uses both.
534. When you stretch the truth, watch out for the snapback.
535. Polygamy would never work in this country. Think of six wives in a kitchenette!
536. A diplomat is a man who puts his best foot forward when he doesn't have a leg to stand on.
537. An economist is one who is uncertain about the future and hazy about the present.
538. A tax cut is the kindest cut of all.
539. Modern furniture is furniture that becomes antique before it's paid for.
540. Forest fires are often caused by tourists. When they're through with the scenery, they burn it.
541. It seems that every year it takes less time to fly across the ocean and longer to drive to work.
542. Marriage would work out better if both sides would operate on a thrifty-thrifty basis.
543. When the pessimist thinks he's taking a chance, the optimist feels he is grasping a great opportunity.
544. A practicing physician is a doctor who says, "If this doesn't cure you, I'll give you something that will."

545. Our problems are alike, except that I don't worry about yours.
546. The word you're able to get in edgewise is apt to be sharp.
547. There are altogether too many people who seem to have a "Do not disturb" sign on their opinions.
548. The shortest path to your happiness is the round-about way of making others happy first.
549. If a care is too small to prompt a prayer, it's too small to be a burden.
550. Faith is never surprised by success.
551. The poorest man in the world is the one who is always wanting more than he has.
552. A pessimist is a guy who crosses his fingers when he says, "Good Morning."
553. Modern music is the kind that puts the "din" in dinner and takes the "rest" out of restaurant.
554. What this country needs is tranquility without tranquilizers.
555. Members of the younger generation are alike in many disrespects.
556. An executive is a man who goes from his air-conditioned office in an air-conditioned car to his air-conditioned club to take a steam bath.
557. The plain fact is that human beings are happy only when they are striving for something worthwhile.
558. Anyone who thinks the automobile has made people lazy never has had to pay for one.
559. When you're inclined to sound off, remember the drum—in spite of all its noise, it is empty!
560. One trouble with the government is that it seems to think the individual owes it a living.
561. What is obviously needed to combat pollution is an automobile engine that runs on garbage.
562. A happy home is one in which each spouse grants the possibility that the other may be right, though neither believes it.
563. Television is a machine that offers people who don't have anything to do a chance to watch people who can't do anything.
564. It's not the difference between people that's the difficulty. It's the indifference.
565. These days they carry you into a hospital fee first.
566. The headache people not only sponsor the news, they encourage it.
567. Just about the time we think we've found a hedge against inflation, someone clips it.
568. Work is the greatest thing in the world, so we should always save some of it for tomorrow.

569. If anything lucky happens to you, don't fail to go and tell it to your friends in order to annoy them.
570. Young married couples start out with wall-to-wall carpeting and back-to-back financing.
571. There is one protest sign understood the world over: the stifled yawn.
572. Only two things are necessary to keep a wife happy. First, let her think she's having her way. Second, let her have it.
573. You can't fool all the people all the time, but some of those super highway interchange signs come pretty close.
574. It seems like the best waiters in restaurants are the customers.
575. The problem of noise will always be a factor in our society so long as there are two sides to any question.
576. Man's life is bound together by family ties, business connections, and golf links.
577. The trouble with people these days is that they want to reach the promised land without going through the wilderness.
578. Most of us like rock and roll music if it is so far away we can't hear it.
579. Will the time ever come when old Santa will stop making house calls?
580. The best gift for the man who has everything is a burglar alarm.
581. Kindness is more than deeds. It is an attitude, an expression, a look, a touch. It is anything that lifts another person.
582. Prejudice is nothing more than an outgrowth of ignorance.
583. The man who remembers what he learned at his mother's knee was probably bent over at the time.
584. One way to keep young boys from getting on the wrong track is to use better switching facilities.
585. There was a time when people who wore blue jeans worked.
586. What a splendid thing it would be if those who lose their tempers could not find them again.
587. A budget helps you pay as you go if you don't go anywhere.
588. Doctors tell us that hating people can cause ulcers, heart attacks, headaches, skin rashes and asthma. It doesn't make the people we hate feel too good either.
589. The number of accidents in the home is rising; people aren't spending enough time there to know their way around.
590. A loose tongue sometimes leads to loose teeth.
591. There's a lot of difference between, "You look like the breath of spring," and "You look like the end of winter."

592. Quite a number of boys were excused from school early on the day of their senior prom. They were having their hair done.

593. Hospitals put both a fellow and his bankroll on the critical list.

594. There is irony in giving your son an expensive guitar—and then finding out that all he wants to sing is a protest against your way of life.

595. A good leader is one who takes a little more than his share of the blame and a little less than his share of credit.

596. Courtship, unlike proper punctuation, is a period before a sentence.

597. One way to make a long story short is by telling it to the elevator operator.

598. Experience is what tells you to watch your step and is what you get if you don't.

599. Most people who switched from cyclamates to saccharine got artificial diabetes.

600. You'll save yourself no end of trouble and sorrow if you think today and talk tomorrow.

601. How often do you hear of a protest march in a communist country?

602. Viewing today's high cost of living, it looks like some of us are pretty lucky to be alive.

603. Isn't it nice that warm weather comes along at the same time the tax collector takes the shirt off your back?

604. One thing you can say for some of today's college students is they are not letting education go to their heads.

605. The price of progress is change and it is taking all we have.

606. Opportunity knocks as often as a man has an ear trained to hear her, an eye trained to see her, a hand trained to grasp her, and a head trained to utilize her.

607. To be seventy years young is sometimes far more cheerful and hopeful than to be forty years old.

608. The employee who will steal FOR his boss will steal FROM his boss.

609. Improve your time, and your time will improve you.

610. Too many try to get something from worship without putting something in.

611. What is really needed is not a forty-hour week but a forty-day month.

612. The devil doesn't care how much good we do, so long as we don't do it today.

613. It makes sense to know where a road is leading before traveling on it.

614. You do not waste time; time wastes you.

615. Time passes quickly. We cannot save it, we cannot buy it. There is nothing we can do about it except to make good use of it as it passes.
616. What a scarcity of news there would be if we all obeyed the Ten Commandments.
617. Poor workmen always find fault with their tools.
618. Character is what we are. Reputation is what we've got the world thinking we are.
619. Children are creatures who disgrace us in public by behaving just like we do at home.
620. Criticism should always leave a person with the feeling that he has been helped.
621. What makes it so hard to get by these days is that our necessities are too luxurious and our luxuries are too necessary.
622. Anyone who doesn't worry about the world situation today ought to have his TV examined.
623. Men tire themselves in pursuit of rest.
624. God tries us with a little to see what we would do with a lot.
625. Scandal, crime, failure make news—but success makes history.
626. Time heals many wounds; it also wounds many heels.
627. Success comes from having the proper aim as well as the right ammunition.
628. The future frightens only those who prefer living in the past.
629. Very few people find a sermon long if it is helpful.
630. The foolish and the dead never change their opinions.
631. Memory is a faculty that reminds you that you've probably forgotten something.
632. You can always tell a self-made man. He either claims the credit or denies the blame.
633. A sneeze is nature's way of enabling a man to interrupt his wife.
634. Fast friends are not made that way.
635. A "peace rally" is as much of a misnomer as a "slumber party."
636. Had you ever noticed that your luck is good if it isn't bad?
637. If you fail to find your place in the sun, at least you'll save on lotion.
638. No matter how many ashtrays you put around your house for a party, someone always puts a cigarette out in something that isn't one.
639. The money we earn from honest labor, most often is spent to impress a neighbor.

640. Middle-age is that time of life when a woman won't tell her age and a man won't act his.
641. Horse sense deserts you when you feel your oats.
642. According to the latest statistics, there are three million Americans who aren't working. And there are even more if you count those with jobs.
643. There are times when silence is the best way to shout at the top of your voice.
644. One reason computers can do more work than humans is that they never have to stop to answer the telephone.
645. Maybe the reason we didn't have so much juvenile delinquency 50 years ago was because we didn't have so many juveniles.
646. Cattlemen are not the only people who like a good looking calf.
647. Approximately 50 percent of the married people in the United States are women.
648. Don't you really feel like a lot of folks actin' foolish these days ain't actin'?
649. All of us like to sign checks—on the back.
650. Next year 3,500,000 kids will turn 16, and 7,000,000 parents will turn pale.
651. If you get more of anything for your dollars these days it's probably bills.
652. The average dinner conversation is a series of cold cuts—her spiced tongue, and his baloney.
653. Fishing is like romance; the next best thing to experiencing it is talking about it.
654. Did you hear about that transportation device guaranteed to cut air pollution over 99 percent? It is called a horse.
655. Any girl who is swept off her feet probably doesn't have big ones.
656. Wisdom is knowing when to speak your mind and when to mind your speech.
657. How did mothers ever learn all the things they warn their daughters not to do?
658. The college campus today is one of the biggest supporters of wild life.
659. Betting on a sure thing is one way of finding out how uncertain life can be.
660. Kindness is the world's greatest unused capital.
661. The surest way to get down to the real nitty-gritty is to eat lunch on the beach.
662. Another form of wastefulness is expenditure of words beyond the income of ideas.
663. In some cities they tear down buildings to save taxes. They might try tearing down some taxes to save buildings.

664. In prosperity men ask too little of God. In adversity, too much.
665. Probably nothing in the world arouses more false hopes than the first four hours of a diet.
666. Sign at library entrance, "Welcome, Silent Majority."
667. An executive is one who never puts off until tomorrow what he can get someone else to do today.
668. A smart politician is one who never throws his hat into the ring until he knows which way the wind is blowing.
669. Profanity is the mark of a conversational cripple.
670. Industry is fortune's right hand and frugality her left.
671. It is sometimes said that society will achieve the kind of education it deserves. Heaven help us if this is so.
672. Advice to public speakers, "When you're done pumpin', let loose of the handle."
673. Since teen-agers are too old to do the things kids do and not old enough to do things adults do, they do things nobody else does.
674. Television does to your mind what cotton candy does to your body. It attracts your attention, makes you want it, and then leaves you with nothing but an empty feeling and a toothache.
675. Exercise doesn't make you nearly as hungry as thinking does—especially thinking about food.
676. Today we have sermonettes by preacherettes for Christianettes.
677. The peace which men seek is not signed at a conference table. It is negotiated in the heart and pursued in daily relationships.
678. A wife is just the opposite of a fisherman; she brags about the ones that got away and complains about the one she caught.
679. The reason some people have so much of nothing is because they expect nothing!
680. He who hesitates these days is honked at.
681. Your best bet is not to make one.
682. More time in God's house will bring about better times in our house.
683. Can you remember when the air used to be clean and sex was dirty?
684. The art of living is the process of getting along with people you do not like.
685. An embezzler is known by the company he clips.
686. You can always tell a man who's head of the house. He's a bachelor.
687. The bulls and the bears aren't nearly as responsible for stock market losses as the bum steers.

688. It's about time for folks to carry this do-it-yourself craze to thinking.
689. The biggest difference between communism and capitalism is plenty.
690. If you'll hunt for the good in the other fellow maybe he'll be able to find some good in you.
691. Humor is a hole that lets the sawdust out of a stuffed shirt.
692. Like its politicians and its wars, society has the teen-agers it deserves.
693. The empty tomb proves Christianity, but an empty pew in worship denies it.
694. It's a crime to catch fish in some lakes, and a miracle in others.
695. Those who court trouble these days will never come out with a hung jury.
696. A suburban mother's role is to deliver children: obstetrically once, and by car forever.
697. You can't get into the Hall of Fame on a pass.
698. Maybe the revolver won the West but the air conditioner made it worth keeping.
699. It's beginning to look as though the safest way to start a day is to go back to bed.
700. History seems to have a way of repeating itself—Nero fiddled and today the melody is played on a guitar.
701. Love is the feeling that makes a woman make a man make a fool of himself.
702. New shoes hurt the most when you have to buy them for the whole family.
703. About all that remains to be shocked these days is a corn field.
704. Some men marry poor girls to settle down, and others marry rich ones to settle up.
705. There's no better diet than eating only as much as you can afford.
706. The truly educated man is that rare individual who can separate reality from illusion.
707. Some people grow up and still remain juvenile.
708. When a fellow is kicking he has only one leg to stand on.
709. These days about all you get for a dollar is a hand waiting for more.
710. Some parents begin with giving in and end with giving up.
711. The guy whose troubles are all behind him is probably a school bus driver.
712. It's not the coffee, but the price of it that keeps folks awake.
713. It's a pity that blight is reducing the yield of corn in the fields instead of on some television shows.

714. In this world there are only two tragedies: One is not getting what one wants, and the other is getting it.
715. Thinking will get you to the foot of the mountain; faith will get you to the top.
716. A well—informed man is one whose wife has just told him what she thinks of him.
717. Early settlers started this country, but it's those who settle on the first of the month that keep it going.
718. One doesn't have to be smart to say things that do.
719. Great opportunities come to those who make the most of small ones.
720. Walking is not an entirely lost art—after all, we do have to get out to the garage by some means.
721. If you are ever asked what our nation stands for, you might answer with two words—TOO MUCH.
722. Most girls bait their hooks for goldfish.
723. The man who wins most of his arguments usually loses most of his friends.
724. A good executive is one who believes that an assistant who does all the work should get at least half the credit.
725. Truth may not be stranger than fiction, but it's a darn sight cleaner.
726. Always look at the brighter side: whenever a car is stolen, it creates another parking place.
727. So many things that broaden the mind also narrows the conscience.
728. Sign on a gas station, "Buzz twice for night service. Then keep your shirt on while I get my pants on."
729. In Spring a young man's fancy turns to love. Nothing is said about a young woman's, possibly because hers is turned to love all year.
730. Getting old is merely a matter of feeling your corns more than you feel your oats.
731. Safety sign in front of school, "Watch out for school children, especially if they are driving cars."
732. These are difficult days for politicians. With the population explosion, they can't even declare themselves for mother-hood without losing some votes.
733. Fools rush in where fools have been before.
734. Few people have good enough sight to see their own faults.
735. It is beginning to look like pork chop prices have gone hog wild.
736. One of the most common disrupters of marital bliss is the choice of where to spend a vacation. What this country needs is an ocean in the mountains.
737. One thing about these dizzy days is that more people are butting in to other people's business than ever before.

738. Anyone who tells you what kind of person he is usually isn't that kind at all.
739. Farming looks mighty easy when you plow with a pencil.
740. It is better to be despised for the right than praised for the wrong.
741. A groom is a fellow about to discover that where there's smoke there's toast.
742. More golden anniversaries would be celebrated if more couples practiced the Golden Rule.
743. Foreign observers say America is no longer a young country—it's reaching meddle-age.
744. Mini-skirt wearers have formed a new organization named, "Daughters of the American Revelation."
745. An Arkansas nitwit recently said, "I could have been a bigger idiot but I lacked ambition."
746. When driving, there are two things that not wearing a seat-belt has brought closer together—this world and the next.
747. People who believe what goes up must come down are sometimes called farmers.
748. An embezzler is one who keeps too much to himself.
749. Spiritual growth soars when we have prayed up, made up and paid up.
750. Modern youth has been tried and found wanting—everything under the sun.
751. Everybody who gets where they are, had to start from where they were.
752. Scientists now tell us the earth is slightly pear-shaped. At one time it was thought to be flat. If this inflation keeps climbing, it may be flat again.
753. Most folks these days have to put out the light to be in the dark.
754. One of the large drug companies has been asked to compound a "pill" to inhibit spending—by Senators.
755. Studies show that modern people are growing taller. But somehow they manage to stay up to their necks in trouble.
756. A kindness done today is the surest way to brighten tomorrow.
757. People who struggle too hard to make both ends meet sometimes have an empty middle.
758. When a husband has the last word the discussion isn't over.
759. The most dangerous way to cross the street is on foot.
760. Said a store owner, "Yes, we have quite a selection of loafers. I'll see if I can get one of them to wait on you."
761. Oil and water mixes better than wives and secretaries.
762. A salesman cannot afford many enemies and cannot have too many friends.

763. The trick is to get education out of politics—and get it into politicians.
764. A hospital is about the only place where one gets stuck for blood going in and bled going out.
765. In the old days, if a kid was in the principal's office, it meant the kid was in trouble. Now it means the principal's in trouble.
766. Rumors without a leg to stand on still have a way of getting around.
767. A bigot is a person who slams his mind in your face.
768. If they really want to beautify our highways, they might remove those tollbooths.
769. When it comes to giving till it hurts, most of us have a very low threshold of pain.
770. It's a happy home where the only scraps are those brushed off the diningroom table.
771. What this country needs are family trees that will produce more lumber and fewer nuts.
772. Some Christians are like trailers—they have to be pulled.
773. A man about to jump off a cliff yelled, "Farewell, cruel environment."
774. Free speech is the kind you get a lot of during a political campaign.
775. Pa with a paddle was about the best aid to education this country ever had.
776. After all is said and done, it looks like more could be done if not so much was said.
777. A fellow now has to pay for cigarettes twice: when he gets them and when they get him.
778. Parents who make a career out of sticking to close family ties seldom sees these relations come unglued.
779. Travel broadens the mind, flattens the finances, and lengthens the conversation.
780. Las Vegas is a wonderful town. You can't beat the climate, the food, or the tables.
781. Behind every argument is someone's ignorance.
782. Anybody who thinks practice makes perfect never tried holding his breath.
783. Your son is at just the right age when the only thing he has on the string is a kite.
784. A man is known by the company he thinks nobody knows he's keeping.
785. To put crime down folks have gotta stop puttin' up with it.
786. You can't pay cash for wisdom. It comes to you on the installment plan.
787. If we all profited by our mistakes millionaires would be commonplace.

788. A filing cabinet is a place where papers sometimes get lost alphabetically.

789. These are the days when two can live as cheaply as one large family used to.

790. It's very touching to hear Yule carolers standing in the smog singing, "It Came upon a Midnight Clear."

791. In today's colleges, the freshmen are smarter than the seniors; everything the seniors have learned is already outmoded.

792. Many folks who are on a fixed income are sure in a bad fix these days.

793. People who recognize that money won't buy happiness are still willing to see if credit cards will do the trick.

794. There's so much air pollution around these days that people are coughing even when they're not at a play or concert.

795. A fellow never knows what he can do until he has to undo something he "done."

796. History books which contain no lies are extremely dull.

797. If women's fashions continue at their present rate, the next creation is likely to be a gownless strap.

798. We like people who agree with us and food that doesn't.

799. Character is man's greatest asset. It should be invested in the best, involved in the important, and inspired by the highest.

800. It requires experience to know how to use it.

801. You should keep all your resolutions secret. That way, nobody knows when you break one.

802. If you can't see good in people, see nothing.

803. In past years some Christmas stockings provided Santa with a few problems; but one wonders next Christmas what may be his reaction to finding panty hose!

804. It will be a great day when everybody who has a job is working.

805. Folks are in a pretty bad fix if they have more dollars than sense.

806. Thinking about income taxes often taxes the mind which is something people once said the Internal Revenue Service couldn't do.

807. A faith worth embracing is a faith worth proclaiming.

808. If postage goes up again, they had better mix tranquilizers with the glue on stamps.

809. It's the thing he learns across his mother's knee that makes a youngster smart.

810. Some people don't mind lying, but they hate inaccuracy.

811. The man who tresspasses another's character, does damage to his own.

812. A success tip: Always seek to excel yourself. Put yourself in competition with yourself each day. Each morning look back over your work of yesterday and try to beat it.

813. Subtlety is the art of saying what you think and getting out of range.

814. Separation of Church and State could hardly be more complete. The church teaches that money isn't everything and the government keeps telling us it is.

815. Psychiatrists say talking helps solve problems—causes 'em, too.

816. The proper pitch for one of these electric guitars is out the window.

817. Maybe the good old days were so good because folks were good.

818. You're an old-timer if you can remember when rock was something you did in a chair.

819. Beware lest your train of thought is just a string of empties.

820. Alimony is repossessed love that one must still pay out on the installment plan.

821. If a man takes his hat off in an elevator, it means he has good manners and hair.

822. Satan hinders prayer, but prayer also hinders Satan.

823. It's a small world—until it comes to driving in from the airport.

824. Used cars are all right as far as they go.

825. There are too many cold wars and hot rods.

826. Automation is a process that gets all the work done while you just sit there. When you were younger, this process was called MOTHER.

827. The Internal Revenue Service, like our Lord, must love poor people—it makes so many of them.

828. You will find that most doctors today will still make house calls, providing you have a telephone there.

829. Tolerance is only another word for indifference.

830. Middle-age is when a man is as young as he feels after trying to prove it.

831. The best things in life may be free but a fellow sure has to fight his way through the crowds to get to them.

832. A business man who came up the hard way observes that about all you can do on a shoe string these days is trip.

833. Faith is the wind that blows the sails of our Ships of Hope toward destinations we desire eventually to reach.

834. Experience is a school where a man learns what a big fool he has been.

835. She was voted the "prettiest girl" month before last; the "most popular" last month; and the most "stuck up" girl in school this month.

836. Having a good reputation is what usually makes people wonder what you're hiding.
837. Money talks, but today's dollar doesn't have cents enough to say very much.
838. Poetry is truth in Sunday clothes.
839. If you think practice makes perfect, you don't have a child taking piano lessons.
840. They tell us to take things as they come—but who can handle them that fast?
841. Someday science may be able to explain why a child can't walk around a puddle.
842. Economists say we may have to de-value the dollar. What do they think Congress has been doing for the past 25 or 30 years?
843. There is some concern about health risks from certain color television sets—and we could add moral risks from some off-color programs.
844. Patience is a minor form of despair disguised as a virtue.
845. One thing can be said for smoking three packs of cigarettes every day. It gives your hands something to do—like shake.
846. There's one consolation in being married to the job. You'll never be divorced from a paycheck.
847. Nothing makes a little knowledge as dangerous as examination time.
848. There's justice for all, but often it isn't equally distributed.
849. Don't worry about your mistakes. Some of the dullest people don't make any.
850. And there's the income tax expert who labeled his office a den of inequity.
851. One housewife to another, "My husband says that I'm what he has left after taxes."
852. Drive with care. Life has no spare.
853. The law of heredity is that all undesirable traits come from the other parent.
854. Nursing a grudge is like arguing with a cop. The more you do it the worse things get.
855. Whether the debt is big or small, inability to pay puts us all in the same category.
856. Time is not an enemy unless you try to kill it.
857. It looks like those folks who are trying to find work for everybody ought to be trying to get everybody to work.
858. Many parents enjoy their children's pets until the pets start having children.
859. A man in Georgia admits to having been so ugly in his infancy that his mother had to borrow a baby to take to church on Sunday.

860. Health rule: Eat like a king for breakfast; a prince for lunch; and a pauper for supper.
861. They say the times are out of joint—but it seems more like a compound fracture.
862. Thanks to air pollution—the breath of Spring has halitosis.
863. All men are honest—until they are faced with a temptation big enough to make them dishonest.
864. We shouldn't object to criticism—if it's favorable.
865. A bore takes his time taking our time.
866. Vulgarity is the broth boiling out of a sick mind.
867. The world keeps finding new ways to do bad things.
868. A young married woman in New Mexico recently sued for divorce. He told her he was a bricklayer when he was only a bank president.
869. Middle-age is when a man realizes he has to mend his ways if he doesn't want to come apart.
870. Analysis of the lunar soil shows about the only thing we can raise on the moon is taxes.
871. Worry is usually only a morbid anticipation of events which never happen.
872. If ignorance is bliss, why aren't more people happy?
873. Some folks who sit around waiting for their ship to come in often find it is a hardship.
874. The best rule in driving through five o'clock traffic is to try and avoid being a part of the six o'clock news.
875. You can never whitewash yourself by blackening others.
876. Seldom does the one who really needs advice ask for it.
877. The biggest drawback to budding love these days is the blooming expense.
878. If there's a skeleton in your closet, it may be because somebody pulled a boner.
879. We are told that manufacturers of aspirin want to sponsor televised sessions of Congress on one of the major networks.
880. Most people have good common sense, but many of them use it only in an emergency or as a last resort.
881. Letting the cat out of the bag is much easier than putting it back.
882. Eagles on dollars are proper and right, because they symbolize the swiftness of flight.
883. The home stretch is trying to make both ends meet.
884. All too often the shortest distance between two points is under construction.
885. We're architects of our fortunes and some of us have strange designs.
886. Many more people are painsgiving than painstaking.

887. Spring represents that transition from the rag weed to the yard weed.
888. Man is the least expensive, all-purpose computing system that can be mass-produced by unskilled labor.
889. You're not too old to learn—unless you are a teen-ager.
890. These are the days when all you can stir up is your coffee.
891. Some fellows spend so much on liquor and women they don't have anything left for luxuries.
892. Perhaps the biggest promissory note that man will ever sign is his marriage license.
893. Television isn't so bad if you do not turn it on.
894. You can take people out of the slums, but it is much better to take the slums out of people.
895. Worry is wonderful if it moves you to do things; corroding if it doesn't.
896. Things always turn out best for the fellow who makes the best of how things turn out.
897. A Texas father says the last bill from his son's college was a bit confusing. He wasn't sure if it was for tuition or bail.
898. Money may not buy happiness, but it sure comes in handy when a fellow gets ready to pay his taxes.
899. A person is constantly called upon to create his own future.
900. Left to themselves, things always go from bad to worse.
901. Do not condemn the judgment of another because it differs from your own. You may both be wrong.
902. The inevitable has happened. An artificial kidney has come down with hepatitis.
903. If a thing is old, it is a sign that it was fit to live. Old families, old customs, old styles survive because they are fit to survive.
904. The woman's work that is never done is getting her husband to help.
905. One thing most family trees have in common is a shady branch.
906. Moonlighting gives one the prospect of a bright future but an awfully dull past.
907. Hospital costs are high, but where else can you get breakfast in bed?
908. Our country needs more conservation and less conversation.
909. Good behavior gets a lot of credit that really belongs to lack of opportunity.
910. A lie can travel around the world while the truth is getting one leg in its pants.
911. To be a success these days a man has to do more than he can do and be better than he is.
912. Philosophy is common sense in a dress suit.

913. The three R's of American schooling are about to be replaced by three C's—cigarettes, cocaine, and cocktails.
914. A cynical husband recently made the following statement, "I never appreciated real happiness until I got married—then it was too late."
915. Don't make any long range plans—such as tomorrow.
916. Advice is somewhat like medicine—the correct dosage works wonders, but an overdose can be disastrous.
917. Prices soar; housewives sore.
918. It is beginning to look like a lot of people want an occupation that doesn't keep them occupied.
919. Economizing is easier when you're broke.
920. The biggest trouble with the human race is that nobody wins it.
921. If we can't win the war against crime, how about a cease fire?
922. When a boy seems bent on marrying, there is usually some girl who is eager to straighten him out.
923. A Chicago psychiatrist received the following card from a patient who was vacationing in Las Vegas, "Having a wonderful time. Wish you were here to tell me why."
924. Our income tax forms should be more realistic by allowing the taxpayer to list Uncle Sam as a dependent.
925. A man has no more character than he can command in a time of crisis.
926. Blessed are our enemies, for they tell us the truth when our friends flatter us.
927. Kindness is a warm breeze in a frigid climate; a radiant heat that melts the icebergs of fear, distrust, and unhappiness.
928. If you are satisfied with yourself you had better change your ideal.
929. An applicant was filling out a long employment form for a well-known southern textile complex. On the line asking, "Length of residence at present address," he wrote, "About forty feet."
930. It might not be opportunity you hear knocking—it could be your spark plugs.
931. Do you remember when the family's meals were carefully thought out instead of thawed out?
932. A poor memory is one requirement for a clear conscience.
933. Some lawyers are just opposite from laundrymen; they lose your suit and then take you to the cleaners.
934. A man should keep his faith in constant repair.
935. Jealousy makes us smaller in the hearts of our friends, weaker in the eyes of our adversaries, and defenseless in the hand of our enemies.

936. Blessed is he who has learned to admire but not envy, to follow but not imitate, to praise but not flatter, and to lead but not to manipulate.
937. Nothing makes youth so bad as having lost it.
938. Some fishermen don't catch anything until they get home.
939. There is a new doll on the market called the welfare doll. You wind it up and it doesn't work.
940. It is better to be alone than in bad company.
941. About the only way Washington will ever stop inflation is to stop inflating.
942. Life may be difficult, but you can sleep one-third of it away.
943. A teen-ager is a person who knows the answer to any problem he doesn't understand.
944. Tact is the fine art of not saying what you think.
945. It looks like businessmen would get along better if they could get more orders from customers and less from government.
946. People are running around in circles trying to make ends meet.
947. There are three ways in which a man can achieve success in this glorious land of ours, He can be rich, famous, or elected.
948. Something that cost $5.00 to buy a few years ago now costs $10.00 to repair.
949. We too often love things and use people when we should be using things and loving people.
950. One benefit of the youth revolt: It's stopped a lot of people from bragging about their kids.
951. A board in the hand is worth two courses in child psychology.
952. The wife who used to complain about dishpan hands is now suffering from push-button fingers.
953. A life worth living has three ingredients. It has a creed—what we believe. It has a code—how we behave. And it has a character—what we become.
954. One thing you can get for a nickel is a cab driver's opinion of you.
955. The mouths of many people seem to have the habit of going on active duty while their brains are on furlough.
956. A mortician advertised as follows: "Use our lay-away plan. Pay now, go later."
957. Americans just don't count their blessings. They're the only people in the world who can afford chairs that vibrate and insist upon cars that don't.
958. Count that day won when, turning on its axis, the earth imposes no additional taxes.

959. Science has produced so many substitutes that it is hard for us to remember what we needed in the first place.
960. The successful man is one who looks outward upon the world, rather than inward upon himself.
961. A doctor says that women can hear better than men. They can also overhear better than men.
962. Middle-age is when a noisy joint is your knee.
963. The Golden Rule is what we want everyone else to practice.
964. Hard cash is the cushion people want to fall back on.
965. Integration can work—just look at Washington, D. C.
966. Maybe what's wrong with our economy is that there ain't any.
967. Watch out for the fellow who says you can't take it with you because he may be trying to take it away from you.
968. There comes a time in the affairs of man that he must take the bull by the tail and face the situation.
969. Psychiatrists say big men make docile husbands—so do big women.
970. Jet planes and superhighways make it easier to visit relatives—especially ancestors.
971. The word, "anger," is only one letter removed from "danger."
972. It's fortunate that we have freedom of speech, but it's unfortunate that the supply usually exceeds the demand.
973. A golddigger is the type of girl who tries to shorten the distance from wink to mink!
974. One trouble with this country is that we have too many people throwing brick and too few laying them.
975. Overweight folks usually watch what they eat closely—all the way from plate to mouth.
976. Actually we wouldn't mind Uncle Sam's tax-bite—if he didn't come back for dessert.
977. Sizes are often deceiving. Sometimes a woman's thumb has a man under it.
978. Might doesn't make right, but it keeps trying.
979. Thanks to jogging, more people are collapsing in perfect health than ever before.
980. An inexcusable mistake is always made by the other fellow.
981. Many a speaker who rises to the occasion stands too long.
982. A compliment is the soft soap that wipes out a dirty look.
983. The meek haven't inherited the earth as yet, but it sure looks like they are supporting it.
984. Maybe what we need today is an installment plan that would let a fellow pay his installments in installments.
985. Sign on a church bulletin board: DO YOU KNOW WHAT AGONY IS? Come in and hear our mixed quartet.

986. Teen-agers today know everything—except the lessons the teacher assigned to them for tomorrow's school day.
987. Antiques are things that one generation buys, the next generation gets rid of and the following generation buys again.
988. A wife can't make her husband do anything—but she can make him wish he had.
989. This is still the land of opportunity. Where else could you afford to have so many things you can't pay for?
990. The word, "alimony," is a contraction of "all his money."
991. When a man forgets himself, he usually does something that everybody else remembers.
992. Inflation is when a fixed income is probably in need of repair.
993. If a man could have half his wishes he'd probably double his troubles.
994. The trouble with being an expert is that you can't turn to anybody else for advice.
995. Some historians say the Egyptians contributed more to civilization than any other people. They invented and popularized soap.
996. Middle-age is when your spring fancy lightly turns to liver pills.
997. The way stores are pushing credit, you'd think C-A-S-H was a dirty four-letter word.
998. When a young man starts right out complaining about his bride's cooking, one of two things will happen: she'll learn better—or he will.
999. Taxes are a state we are deeply in the heart of.
1000. Humility is the ability to be slightly embarrassed when people tell you how wonderful you are.
1001. If our faith cannot move mountains, at least it ought to climb them.
1002. The human mind was intended for a storehouse, not a waste basket.
1003. An educated fool is a bigger fool than an ignorant one.
1004. The church that is always "chewing the rag" isn't very well fed.
1005. Sympathy is YOUR pain in MY heart.
1006. They who think money will do anything will do anything for money.
1007. We like the man who says what he thinks—that is, when he agrees with us.
1008. Do you suppose Little Red Riding Hood's mother was called Mother Hood?
1009. Better a blush on the face than a blot in the heart.

1010. With every sin the devil also provides an excuse.
1011. Enthusiasm is as contagious as the measles and as powerful as dynamite.
1012. The function of fear is to warn us of danger, not to make us afraid to face it.
1013. We are always too busy to visit the sick but never too busy to serve as a pall-bearer.
1014. Forgiveness saves the expense of anger, the cost of hatred, and the waste of energy.
1015. Almost everybody smokes the pipe of peace but few inhale.
1016. If you make the church important, it is quite likely to return the favor.
1017. There are three stages in American history: the passing of the Indian, the passing of the buffalo, and the passing of the buck.
1018. Good examples have twice the value of good advice.
1019. Garments of righteousness never go out of style.
1020. Going to bed can cure half the world's ills—and getting up the other half.
1021. It takes a second-hand person to deliver first-hand gossip.
1022. The really happy man is one who can enjoy the scenery when on a detour.
1023. Instead of broadcasting so much, why not try tuning in at intervals?
1024. The search for happiness is one of the chief sources of unhappiness.
1025. It's hard to sling mud with clean hands.
1026. The most pointed remarks often come from blunt people.
1027. Respectable vices are doubly dangerous.
1028. Many a retired husband becomes his wife's full-time job.
1029. Don't cheat the Lord and call it economy.
1030. What you don't owe won't hurt you.
1031. An actor is a man who tries to be everything but himself.
1032. One can conquer a bad habit easier today than tomorrow.
1033. Every man has his price and every woman her figure.
1034. The time has now come when you can borrow enough to get out of debt.
1035. Half our troubles come in wanting our way; the other half comes in getting it.
1036. It seems that some people have RUMORTISM.
1037. A girl is not necessarily an artist just because she paints and chisels.
1038. The elevator man is the only one with the right to run anyone down.
1039. An optimist thinks this is a great world; a pessimist is afraid the optimist is right.

1040. A quitter never wins; a winner never quits.
1041. What happens seldom bothers us as much as what might happen.
1042. You don't have time to criticize when you harmonize, sympathize, and evangelize.
1043. Some think God is like medicine; you don't need Him when you are well.
1044. The worst indigestion comes in eating your own words.
1045. He who makes the most noise about problems does the least about them.
1046. Do not become broadminded from shallow thinking.
1047. The world is full of people making a good living but poor lives.
1048. Heads, hearts, and hands could settle the world's problems better than arms.
1049. Success makes failures out of too many people.
1050. Evil often triumphs but it can never conquer.
1051. A poor listener seldom hears a good sermon.
1052. Don't trust your wife's judgment—just look at whom she married!
1053. He is my friend who believes in me, stands up for me, is candid with me, and loyal to me.
1054. Happiness makes up in height for what it lacks in length.
1055. Never pass on curve or hill—if the cops don't get you the mortician will.
1056. Laws are man's guidelines but unfortunately too many try to read between them.
1057. Forgetfulness is a virtue only when you forget the grievances you have against other people.
1058. If it weren't for betting on horses, some people wouldn't contribute to anything.
1059. You're prejudiced when you weigh the facts with your thumb on the scale.
1060. Making marriage work is like running a farm—you have to start all over each day.
1061. Example is a language all men can read.
1062. A smile is the welcome mat at the doorway of kindness.
1063. Christmas is becoming a race to see whether your feet or your money gives out first.
1064. There is more to life than increasing its speed.
1065. The tragedy of life is what dies inside a man while he lives.
1066. In America, 94 percent of all homes contain at least one television set, but only 85 percent have bathtubs. This proves that more brains are being washed than bodies.
1067. The right to protest is the right to persuade, not the right to paralyze.

1068. There are two ways to be rich: One is the abundance of your possessions and the other in the fewness of your wants.
1069. The hardest victory of all is a victory over self.
1070. Happiness keeps best when kept in circulation.
1071. Recipe for salad from the "Hippie Cook Book": Cut up lettuce, cucumbers, green peppers and tomatoes. Add a little marijuna and let the salad toss itself."
1072. To err is human—to really foul things up requires a computer.
1073. George Washington was the first in war, first in peace, and first to wear a wig and white stretch pants with boots.
1074. A test of any man's character is how he takes praise.
1075. The yoke of God does not fit stiff necks.
1076. Many have ability, but no stability.
1077. A trusted friend is a sea of sincerity, a continent of concern, a universe of understanding, and a galaxy of generosity.
1078. Man has learned to fly like a bird and swim like a fish—he just needs to learn to live like a man.
1079. A withered soul in a healthy body is only a live corpse.
1080. It is unthinkable to expect a child to listen to your advice, and ignore your example.
1081. It's that little difference in each of us that is the big difference.
1082. When a man gets too big for his "britches" his hat doesn't fit either.
1083. Humility makes a man feel smaller as he becomes greater.
1084. One important way for us to help our children grow up is for us to grow up first.
1085. It's hard to sell a product you don't use and religion you don't live.
1086. About the only way a middle-aged woman can hold her school-girl figure is in fond memory.
1087. You can tell what a man is by what he does when he hasn't anything to do.
1088. A man's best boss is a well-trained conscience.
1089. Some people seem to think a fertile mind requires a lot of dirt.
1090. Gossip is something negative that is developed and then enlarged.
1091. Isn't it strange that nobody ever goes to jail for waging wars, or advocating them, but the jails are filled with those who want peace?
1092. Engineers are trying to build a car that will stop smoking— all of us would like to find one that will stop drinking.

1093. Man once subscribed to the theory of male superiority, then woman cancelled his subscription.

1094. The Lord helps those who help themselves. All the others seem to contact the government.

1095. About the best way to grow old is not to be in too much of a hurry about it.

1096. It's hard for a child to live right when he has never seen it done.

1097. Religion is what you do FOR people, not TO people.

1098. One of the hardest things to live down is the time a fellow spends living it up.

1099. A true leader faces the music even when he dislikes the tune.

1100. We have freedom in this country; even the freedom to make fools of ourselves.

1101. A marriage is on solid footing if the parties involved laugh together daily.

1102. Some folks claim that plenty of practice is supposed to make a task easier, but it doesn't seem to help during tax paying time.

1103. A psychologist says, "Don't argue with a tired woman." That's safer, though, than arguing with a rested one.

1104. Many freeways have three lanes: A left lane, a right lane, and the one you're in when you see your exit.

1105. There is little chance for people to get together as long as most of us want to be in the back of the church, the front of the bus, and the middle of the road.

1106. The trouble with being pleasant is that people think you're a hypocrite.

1107. Anybody with a finger in every pie is apt to have sticky fingers.

1108. Embezzling is a matter of negotiating a loan unilaterally.

1109. To err is human; to forget, routine.

1110. A Communist country is free to determine its own future path but it is not free to depart from Communism.

1111. All men are born equal—but some get married.

1112. The best tranquilizer is a clear conscience.

1113. If we paid no more attention to our plants than we do our children we would live in a jungle.

1114. He who forgets the language of gratitude can never be on speaking terms with happiness.

1115. You are expected to make good—not to make excuses.

1116. We can live on less when we have more to live for.

1117. Dollars go farther when accompanied by sense.

1118. He knew not what to say, and so he swore.

1119. If a thing goes without saying—let it go.

1120. The radiant Christian is more concerned with carrying his cross than with complaining about his callouses. He remembers the harvests, not the hardships. He thinks about his friends, not his failures. He talks more about his blessings than his backaches, more about his opportunities than his operations.
1121. Man has always fought fiercely to preserve his ignorance.
1122. Home is where the mortgage is.
1123. Our aim should be service, not success.
1124. Zeal without tolerance is fanaticism.
1125. Politeness is like an air cushion. There may be nothing in it, but it eases the jolts.
1126. Doctor at a Baptist hospital, "We do have a heart transplant available, sir, but it belonged to a Methodist."
1127. If man is a little lower than the angels, the angels should be ashamed of themselves.
1128. The Rock and Roll bands are good and loud—but not loud and good.
1129. When will they stop obstructing the nation's billboards with scenic highways?
1130. Father Time grants no rebate for wasted hours.
1131. By improving yourself is the world made better.
1132. If you have nothing to be thankful for, make up your mind that there is something wrong with you.
1133. Happiness is in the heart, not in the circumstances.
1134. The Christmas spirit that goes out with the dried-up Christmas tree is just as worthless.
1135. Every family tree has some sap in it.
1136. Think! It may be a new experience.
1137. Wishing doesn't make it so.
1138. Not what we have, but what we enjoy constitutes our abundance.
1139. You never know how many friends you have until you own a cottage on the beach.
1140. The world will never be the dwelling place of peace till peace has found a home in the heart of each and every man.
1141. Money won't buy happiness but it will keep a person from having to take misery on an empty stomach.
1142. Buying cheap merchandise to save money is like stopping the clock to save time.
1143. If you think time heals, try sitting it out in a doctor's office.
1144. Service is the rent we pay for the space we occupy in this world.
1145. You can't leave footprints on the sands of time if you don't keep your feet on the ground.

1146. A timid man said to his wife, "We're not going out to-night—and that's semi-final."
1147. Our choice of friends affects our reputation; our choice of thoughts shapes our character.
1148. When all else is lost, the future still remains.
1149. If you cannot do great things, do small things in a great way.
1150. December brings out warm clothes and rosy cheeks while January brings the Internal Revenue Service and some red faces.
1151. What we do not solve today will baffle our children tomorrow.
1152. A lot of folks are not interested in seeing inflation slowed down, they want it backed up.
1153. It is pretty obvious why the husbands of the ten best-dressed women are not on the list of the ten best-dressed men.
1154. Home is a place where you don't have to stifle a yawn and try to cover it up with a smile.
1155. Perhaps the best Yuletide decoration is being wreathed in smiles.
1156. Money seldom goes to a man's head because it has already gone for taxes.
1157. Procrastination is the thief of time, and so is every other big word.
1158. The secret of longevity for bank accounts has been found—month to month resuscitation.
1159. Some young men seem to have dentists confused with barbers—they see their barber twice a year.
1160. Rioters are a minority who refuse to believe the majority have rights too.
1161. If it is true that folks think best on their feet, there must be a lot of people sitting around these days.
1162. It is often difficult for children to understand the innocence of their parents.
1163. A very cultured person is one who can bore you on any subject.
1164. Our ship probably would come in much sooner if we'd only swim out to meet it.
1165. There's no tax on brains—the take would be too small.
1166. Free advice may prove to be the costliest kind.
1167. No person will have occasion to complain of the want of time who never loses any.
1168. Look at it this way—it may be tough to pay over two dollars for a pound of steak. But the less you pay, the tougher it gets.

1169. You never know what some folks will say next and neither do they.

1170. A problem not worth praying about is not worth worrying about.

1171. Why is it that when a fellow's cup of happiness is full, some jerk will come along and nudge his elbow?

1172. Too many people look upon democracy as a chance to push other people around for their own personal benefit.

1173. Running down our friends is the quickest way to run them off.

1174. Profanity is the use of strong words by weak people.

1175. If a man is too lazy to think for himself, he should get married.

1176. Any more deductions in our take-home pay and we won't have a home to take it to.

1177. Some people think religion, like aspirin, should be taken only to relieve pain.

1178. Middle-age is when you're not inclined to exercise anything but caution.

1179. Beware of fate—it loves to take advantage of anyone who believes in it.

1180. A man can build a staunch reputation for honesty by admitting he was in error, especially when he gets caught at it.

1181. Use silence to please—never to punish.

1182. You never realize what a good memory you have until you try to forget.

1183. The best way to keep from worrying is to keep your mind off your thoughts.

1184. Modesty is the triumph of mind over flatter.

1185. These days about the only thing you can be sure of getting for a nickel is five pennies.

1186. There are worse things than death—take life, for instance.

1187. It's awfully easy for people to run into debt, but most folks have to crawl out.

1188. Wouldn't it be a good idea to open a few discount hospitals?

1189. When you make two people happy, one of them is apt to be you.

1190. A man can acquire an ordinary size ulcer at the office, but the larger ones are more often homegrown.

1191. We are all manufacturers in a way—making good, making trouble, or making excuses.

1192. Faith is the magic, vital formula that supplies starch to the spine.

1193. Talk is cheap because the supply is always greater than the demand.

1194. Hard work is the price that must be paid for real success.

1195. Why does it always seem that our blessings can be counted on our fingers, while for all our troubles, we need a computer?

1196. If a man doesn't get happier as he gets older, he hasn't learned what he should along the way.

1197. With today's pollution, all bridges are over troubled waters.

1198. A good wife is one who believes the husband who does all the work should get at least half the credit.

1199. It's a funny thing about some folks. They don't want to be treated like everybody else—they want to be treated better.

1200. Discretion is putting two and two together and keeping your mouth shut.

1201. Happiness is nothing more than good health and a poor memory.

1202. Doing nothing is not the best. How are we going to quit and rest?

1203. Love may make the world go 'round but money pays the way.

1204. It looks like a lot of folks are in a rat race these days and the worst part of it is that a lot of the rats are winning.

1205. In today's society you have to be a little crazy to keep from going insane.

1206. New Years is when some folks drop in for a call and others call in for a drop.

1207. Space suits for the moon walk cost $50,000. For that kind of money we could have sent Liberace.

1208. Happiness, at its best, is based upon relationships and not upon possessions.

1209. If at first you don't succeed, find out WHY before you try again.

1210. A gossip is one who can give you all the details without knowing any of the facts.

1211. One of the big disappointments in this life is to discover that the man who writes the advertising for the bank is not the same guy who makes the loans.

1212. Nothing makes a child as smart as having grandparents.

1213. Sending your child to college is like sending your clothes to the laundry. You get out what you put in, but you don't always recognize it.

1214. It's a man's world, but women run it by making men THINK they do.

1215. Anyone who thinks dirt is cheap never looked for a lot to build a house on.

1216. Folks who fly into a rage always make a bad landing.

1217. A nurse is a woman whose business is to make sickness a pleasure.

1218. Aviation won't really be safe until they do away with the ride to the airport.
1219. It takes a heap of payments to make a house a home.
1220. An overdose of praise is like ten lumps of sugar in coffee; only a few people can swallow it.
1221. In many ways the past 200 years of our history has changed from one of independence to government dependence.
1222. Veterinarians now prescribe birth control pills for dogs—it's a part of an anti-litter campaign.
1223. When you go on a diet, the first thing you lose is your temper.
1224. Old salesmen never die—they just get out of commission.
1225. The first thing a pickpocket learns is to stay away from a man with two kids in college.
1226. Christmas Eve is when you stay in to see how you come out.
1227. We crucify ourselves between two thieves: regret for yesterday and fear of tomorrow.
1228. Instant replay is when your wife finds out you haven't been listening.
1229. Anyone who thinks hard work will never hurt you never had to pay to have it done.
1230. It's fine for a fellow to do things for others but he shouldn't leave himself undone.
1231. The way some people find fault you'd think there was a reward for it.
1232. Many of us feel that when our ship comes in—there'll probably be a dock strike on.
1233. There is an argument going around that the premiums on our foreign policy are running too high.
1234. You can't purify the water in the well by painting the pump.
1235. Every girl has the right to be ugly, but some have abused the privilege.
1236. Anybody who thinks money won't buy happiness has never tried spending it on somebody else.
1237. It seems that some folks have no use for people they can't use.
1238. To a parent, a miracle drug is medicine the kids will take without screaming.
1239. The dismaying thing is not what man descended from, but what he's descending to.
1240. Your reputation can be damaged by the opinions of others. Only you yourself can damage your character.
1241. A newlywed couple shouldn't expect the first few meals to be perfect. After all, it takes time to find the right restaurant.

1242. The fellow who put knobs on gadgets ought to swap jobs with those who screw lids on jars.

1243. There is plenty of money in this country, but the trouble is everybody owes it to somebody else.

1244. The Bible finds us where we are, and, if permitted, takes us where we ought to go.

1245. Santa comes down the chimney and our money goes down the drain.

1246. Heaven help us if we discover other planets are inhabited—think of the increase in our Foreign Aid.

1247. Never invite trouble; it will accept the invitation every time.

1248. One of the saddest things about modern life is the number of people who are spending money they haven't got, for things they don't want, to impress people they can't stand the sight of.

1249. A conversation is like a good meal. You should leave it just before you have had enough.

1250. We have observed that many of the "self-made" men made their heads a bit oversize.

1251. Loyalty is the inheritance tax we should be willing to pay on our American heritage.

1252. A fellow who practices what he preaches has to be careful what he preaches.

1253. The best time for name-dropping is when making a list of people we don't like.

1254. Obstacles are those terrifying things we see when we take our eyes off the goal.

1255. Times are changing. When a man gets mad at his wife now, he goes to his club. In the old days he just reached for it.

1256. Nothing seems to slow you down as much as pushing your luck.

1257. Young people these days will go almost any place for exercise as long as they don't have to walk.

1258. The wise man uses mouth less, eyes more, ears more, and knows more.

1259. Whenever Uncle Sam arrives at an international conference, he is invited to draw up a check and sit down.

1260. When the wife suggests going for a spin, she probably has her revolving charge account in mind.

1261. The thing raised most abundantly in the United States is taxes.

1262. They're adding a new traffic light to the standard group of red, amber and green. If you have an accident, this one squirts iodine.

1263. Advice to some people: If you had your life to live over—don't do it.

1264. The most difficult secret for a man to keep is his own opinion of himself.
1265. Experience enables you to recognize a mistake the next time you make it.
1266. Nothing makes time pass faster than vacations and short-term loans.
1267. Most of us find that it's hard to take advice from people who need it more than we do.
1268. It annoys a housewife to have friends drop in and find the house looking as it usually does.
1269. Remember this, your relatives had no choice in the matter either.
1270. No one has more faith than the person who plays a slot machine.
1271. Almost every child would learn to write sooner if allowed to do his homework on wet cement.
1272. Advice to hunters: Do not get loaded when your gun is.
1273. Bureaucrats live on the fat of the land while the rest of us stay skinny laboring to pay their salaries.
1274. We have learned how to lengthen life but not how to deepen it.
1275. If something goes wrong, it is more important to talk about who will fix it than to talk about who is to blame.
1276. A loafer is a man who tries to make both week—ends meet.
1277. Some people won't take it with them because they didn't save any to take.
1278. It is Christmas in the heart that puts Christmas in the air.
1279. There should be more pleasure in getting into trouble—it's so hard to get out.
1280. If our youth are to bring about peace in tomorrow's world, they must be exposed to peace in today's homes.
1281. Experience is the training that enables you to get along without education.
1282. A lot of people are putting off until tomorrow things they put off the day before.
1283. Our boasted "progress" has landed us, not in Paradise, but in pandemonium.
1284. Any father who complains he is spending thousands for his daughter's wedding isn't complaining—he's bragging.
1285. The thing we don't like about farming is that soil rhymes with toil.
1286. A lot more children would take after their parents if they knew where they went.
1287. Teen-agers are young people who get too much of everything—including criticism.
1288. A man's achievement in business depends partly on whether he keeps his mind or his feet on the desk.

1289. You can fool all the people some of the time, but you can fool yourself all the time.

1290. If we learn by doing things, a lot of people are going to keep on being ignorant.

1291. Experience is the best teacher, but not the prettiest.

1292. It's always good fishing before you get there and after you leave.

1293. Education is what parents get when the children are home from school on vacation.

1294. Many a family argument has been saved by the doorbell or telephone.

1295. The person who agrees with you completely at all times is probably not worth talking to.

1296. You get out of a mirror what you put into it and out of a scale what you put on it.

1297. We like the fellow who is reasonable and does things our way.

1298. It may be bad to talk when your mouth is full, but it isn't too good either when your head is empty.

1299. The best known popular sport today is running into debt.

1300. Nowadays we spend so much on luxuries we can't afford the necessities.

1301. A scientist says even pure-looking air has dirt suspended in it. He apparently has a radio and television.

1302. Tip on saving money: Just forget from whom you borrowed it.

1303. To have average intelligence is to be less stupid than half of the people, and more stupid than the other half.

1304. In the old days history was made for a tenth of what it costs today.

1305. First, men fight for freedom, and then make laws gradually to take it away.

1306. Secrets are a burden. That's the reason we are so anxious to have somebody help us carry them.

1307. A newspaper says it's dangerous for a young man to propose while he is driving a car. It's dangerous anywhere, brother.

1308. Every nation finds it difficult to balance a budget at the end of a sword.

1309. It is not a matter of WHO is right but WHAT is right.

1310. We Americans are the few people in the world who have to ask, "How can I reduce?" and, "Where can I park?"

1311. Success would be a little more attractive if successful men seemed happier.

1312. Nothing conceals your laurels as much as resting on them.

1313. The flattery that gets you nowhere is what you listen to.

1314. It's bad to act like a fool, but it's worse when you're not acting.
1315. One headlight is enough if the other driver guesses correctly which side it is on.
1316. A patriot is a person who saves enough of his salary each week to pay his income tax.
1317. Well-dressed ignorance often goes a long way.
1318. A new Beatitude might well read, "Blessed are the young, for they shall inherit the national debt."
1319. The latest class of underprivileged children are those whose parents own two cars but no speedboat.
1320. In West Germany, so many people are injured by falling out of bed that one physician recommends that beds be made with safety belts.
1321. The thing you learn from experience is that you can't make very much money without working.
1322. That which is given to us by circumstances, accident, or chance can be taken away by the same means. That which we have BECOME is eternal.
1323. It is a principle of law well established that an automobile is not inherently a dangerous machine. It is not the ferocity of automobiles that is to be feared but the ferocity of those who drive them.
1324. Flirtation is paying attention without intention.
1325. Cocktail lounges are half-lit to match the patrons.
1326. Floating church members usually make a sinking church.
1327. The stomach is a tough organ. Many a man has survived eating up to 1000 civic luncheons.
1328. In the old days children were necessities and automobiles luxuries. Now they're reversed.
1329. Progress may have been all right for a while but it sure looks like it has gone on too long.
1330. Forgiveness is the quality of heart that forgets the injury and pardons the offender.
1331. The remarkable thing about most of us is our ability to live beyond our income.
1332. It is not only a man's sins, but his creditors who find him out.
1333. It's getting to where even taxpayers' patience is being taxed.
1334. At least smog enables you to see what you breathe.
1335. The work some people do is so secret they don't know what they're doing.
1336. A little knowledge that acts is worth infinitely more than much knowledge that is idle.
1337. LOVE—may it last all your life!

1338. If men ever learn to control the weather they will sure limit the conversation for a lot of people.
1339. So far, nobody has invented an intelligence test equal to keeping one's mouth shut.
1340. Teen-age boys can't save any money. What they save on haircuts they spend on hair spray.
1341. One secretary to another, "You'll love it here after you once accept the fact there is absolutely no chance for advancement, raises, or marriage."
1342. Americans are getting bigger, a fact which has filtered through to everybody except the people who mark off seats in the football stadium.
1343. Forgiveness, like dimming our headlights, is more effective when we take the initiative.
1344. That is a good book which is opened with expectation, and closed with delight and profit.
1345. Any child who gets raised by the book is probably a first addition.
1346. A celebrity is an ordinary person with a good press agent.
1347. These auto safety tests may be all right to get rattletraps off the highways, but what about the rattle-brains?
1348. We cannot drift into success, loaf our way into achievement, or daydream into eminence.
1349. Today is the first day of the rest of your life.
1350. An idea may be dressed in attractive words and still be stupid.
1351. A fellow's mistakes always bother him, especially when he realizes he's too old to repeat them.
1352. You can study your reflection in a mirror and still really not know how you look to others.
1353. At present prices, who can afford a depression?
1354. All butchers don't weigh their thumb with your meat. Some use a finger.
1355. The Russians have been able to use the space in the skies and the space in the empty heads of many Americans.
1356. One boy on his feet is worth two on their seat.
1357. A happy marriage is the union of two good forgivers.
1358. Many seem allergic to food for thought.
1359. One reason experience is such a great teacher is that she doesn't allow dropouts.
1360. Your stomach can be full but not your mind.
1361. Some people can hold a horse better than they can hold their tongues.
1362. By the time one is old enough to know better, he thinks he is smart enough not to be caught at it.
1363. If we could see ourselves as others see us we'd deny it.

1364. Children are like airplanes; we only hear of the ones that crashed.
1365. Humility makes a man feel smaller as he becomes greater.
1366. Judging by the way some church members live, they need fire insurance.
1367. Christmas is a time when a lot of others besides Santa find themselves in the red.
1368. Our best investment is not in funds but friends.
1369. Wife to husband, "I took one of those compatibility tests in a magazine today and you flunked."
1370. It means you are ahead when you are kicked from the rear.
1371. He who cannot lead and will not follow at least makes a dandy roadblock.
1372. Preachers are determined—if they don't get on your toes they get in your hair.
1373. The man with push will pass the man with pull.
1374. Perhaps the income tax should have been named the outgo tax.
1375. To handle yourself, use your head; to handle others, use your heart.
1376. Mental cases hardest to cure are those who are crazy about themselves.
1377. The entrance to trouble is wide, but the exit is narrow.
1378. The most difficult thing to open is a closed mind.
1379. Adam's first day was the longest—No Eve.
1380. A friend you have to buy is not worth what you paid for him.
1381. Since most sins are pretty expensive it looks like folks would behave themselves and save the difference.
1382. He who carries a tale makes a monkey of himself.
1383. America, the land of opportunity! Where else can one spend so much for so little?
1384. If you think women can't take a joke, look at the husbands they have!
1385. Many people don't mind going to work—it's the long wait until quitting time that's so irritating.
1386. Resort hotels are often surrounded by tropical plants—mostly outstretched palms.
1387. It is true that some days are difficult, but can you remember any day in the past that you failed to survive?
1388. Farmers are so closely inspected by the Federal government that a young country lad hesitates to sow any wild oats.
1389. A fair-weather friend is one who is always around when he needs you.
1390. Children always know when there is company in the living room—they can hear their mother laughing at their father's jokes.

1391. Most of us spend a lot of time and effort crossing bridges to which we never come.
1392. Most things that make us sigh and fret are those things that haven't happened yet.
1393. The best gift around a Christmas tree is the presence of a family all wrapped up in each other.
1394. A man who lives for himself is ruined by the company he keeps.
1395. There is only one endeavor in which you can successfully start at the top, and that's digging a well.
1396. If car insurance rates get any higher, it'll be easier to pay cash for the car and finance the insurance premium.
1397. The little boy sitting beside you will come through if you'll give him a shirt tail to hang onto and have that shirt tail there every time he reaches for it.
1398. A man is not bright because he burns the candle at both ends.
1399. Spiritual cancer cannot be cured by quacks.
1400. If it is the clowns you like to see at a circus, you don't have to go to the circus.
1401. There is a lot of good advice floating around that is as good as new—because it has never been used.
1402. It takes some people a long time to get nothing done.
1403. He who boasts of being self-made relieves the Lord of a lot of responsibility.
1404. Talking that is too long is generally the result of thinking that wasn't long enough.
1405. When a man feels he is utterly useless, he is.
1406. The human tongue was intended for a divine organ, but the devil often plays upon it.
1407. We ought to be thankful that we are living in a country where folks can say what they think without thinking.
1408. Some churches grow by leaps and bounds—backwards.
1409. What's giving you ulcers may be something you hate.
1410. Tact is the ability to describe others as they see themselves.
1411. We can't all swing the baton; some of us must play second fiddle.
1412. The color of a man's skin isn't as important as the color of his stories.
1413. Our Lord cannot go forth to war with an army of tin soldiers.
1414. Lying covers a multitude of sins—temporarily.
1415. Most of us hate to see a poor loser—or a rich winner.
1416. The trouble with the world is that so many people who stand up for their rights fall down miserably on their duties.
1417. The main thing that comes to the man who waits is regret for having waited.

1418. Don't air your prejudices; smother them.
1419. Some family trees seem to produce a variety of nuts.
1420. Praise makes good men better and bad men worse.
1421. The religion of some people is like the merry-go-round: it doesn't get them anywhere.
1422. One's own faults are not minimized by magnifying the faults of others.
1423. An eminent scientist has announced that in his opinion intelligent life is possible on several of the planets— including the earth.
1424. When people pay as they go they ought to be sure they have enough to get back.
1425. You don't have to be much of a musician to toot your own horn.
1426. There's no point in going on a diet if you have to starve to death to live longer.
1427. The greatest talkers usually have the least to say.
1428. If you think you haven't very much to be thankful for, be thankful for some of the things you don't have.
1429. Boys will be boys, and so will a lot of grown men.
1430. It's better to do good than to do people.
1431. Nothing cooks a fellow's goose quicker than a red hot temper.
1432. Most folks can save a little dough if they try, but it's hard to find anything a little dough will buy.
1433. The hardest job that people have to do is to move religion from their throats to their muscles.
1434. Though divided by creeds we can unite with deeds.
1435. It is easy to tell one lie, but hard to tell but one.
1436. Illicit love isn't much fun once it gets into court.
1437. What this country seems to need is less labor-saving devices and better labor on the devices we now have.
1438. One gallon of gas plus one pint of booze often adds up to a funeral.
1439. We may not be able to define the word CHRISTIAN, but the world knows one when it sees one.
1440. Two great tests of character are wealth and poverty.
1441. It would be better if the overstuffed things in homes were confined to furniture.
1442. The price of wheat rises and falls. The price of "wild oats" remains high.
1443. More homes are destroyed by fusses than by funerals or fires.
1444. The devil also loves a cheerful giver—if he is the receiver.
1445. Don't just SAY the Lord's prayer. Pray it.
1446. A paratrooper is constantly climbing down trees he never climbed up.

1447. Some big executives have computers to do their thinking for them. Some just have wives.
1448. No one knows the exact age of the world, but it certainly is old enough to know better.
1449. Get ready for Eternity. You are going to spend a lot of time there.
1450. The poorest way to face life is to face it with a sneer.
1451. No man is rich enough to buy back his past.
1452. Don't set out for a thrill and wind up with a thud.
1453. The world owes you a living, but only when you have earned it.
1454. If there were more self-starters, the boss wouldn't be a crank.
1455. Easy street has a dead end.
1456. If a man cannot be a gentleman where he is, he cannot be a gentleman anywhere.
1457. The rich and the poor look alike soon after the funeral.
1458. It's easy to have a balanced personality. Just forget your troubles as easily as you do your blessings.
1459. Life does not offer us its best on easy terms.
1460. Wouldn't it be wonderful if the Internal Revenue Service gave us the guarantee, "Money back if not satisfied"?
1461. Snap judgment would be all right if it didn't come un-snapped so often.
1462. If the politicians in Washington keep on increasing foreign aid, it won't be long before we won't have a friend in the world.
1463. To take a great weight off your mind, try discarding your halo.
1464. All some people have ready for a rainy day is a freshly washed car.
1465. A white collar man is one who carries his lunch in a briefcase instead of a lunch basket.
1466. Her birthday cake had so many candles on it she was fined for air pollution.
1467. If it weren't for picketing, some Americans wouldn't walk at all.
1468. A single girl is always on the lookout for some man who would be willing to perform a name transplant.
1469. If you wish to dwell in the house of many mansions, you must make your reservation in advance.
1470. Life begins at 40, but you'll miss a lot if you wait that long.
1471. Life has become a struggle between keeping your weight down and your spirits up.
1472. Actually, a real argument is when two people are trying to get in the last word first.

1473. Washington is the seat of government, and the taxpayer is the pants pocket.

1474. Are you a thoughtful doubter—or a doubtful thinker?

1475. The fellow who spends today bragging about what he is going to do tomorrow, probably did the same thing yesterday.

1476. A psychologist recently said that old age is imaginary—it's just in the head. Maybe so, but it hits some people in the legs first.

1477. Most husbands want a wife they can love, honor and display.

1478. God has been around a mighty long time and intends to stay.

1479. The hardest burdens in life to bear are the things that might happen but usually don't.

1480. A sin takes on new and real terrors when there seems to be a chance that it is going to be found out.

1481. When we stop to think that it requires dirt to grow things we better understand why gossip thrives.

1482. The human jaw is shrinking in size, but not from lack of exercise.

1483. Cheer up! There's nothing wrong with this country that a miracle couldn't cure.

1484. Diplomacy is the art of saying, "nice doggy," until you can find a rock.

1485. Formerly a man wondered if he could afford to marry; now he wonders if he can get along without a working wife.

1486. Nothing makes in-laws so exasperating as being yours.

1487. Some of us can remember when an "oil slick" was what a fellow did to his hair.

1488. There are three kinds of traffic problems: urban, suburban, and bourbon.

1489. The only person who listens to both sides of a family argument is the one in the next apartment.

1490. Have you ever noticed that most knocking is done by folks who don't know how to ring the bell?

1491. It is better that the drunkard be in the gutter than behind a steering wheel.

1492. The darkest hour is only 60 minutes long.

1493. You don't have to explain something you haven't said.

1494. Why don't men who dislike the church move to where there is not one?

1495. Bear in mind that children of all ages have one thing in common—they close their eyes to advice and open their eyes to example.

1496. When a man wants to believe something, it doesn't take much to convince him.

1497. An excuse is a thin skin of falsehood stretched tightly over a bald-faced lie.

1498. A man in Kentucky recently liberated his wife, but she wouldn't go.

1499. Weak men catch trouble by the horns and opportunity by the tail.

1500. A person gets paid for using his brains—not for having them.

1501. The best substitute for experience is being 18 years old.

1502. It sure is nice to sit before a roaring fire in the living room on nippy evenings—that is, if you have a fireplace.

1503. The key to lasting peace is to rely less on arms and more on heads.

1504. No words are quite as pleasing as one's own praise.

1505. Every time a man smiles, it seems to add something to his life.

1506. The tightest sticking things in government bureaus are the salary drawers.

1507. Health is wealth—and it's tax free.

1508. When you listen to a political speech, it's like shooting at a target—you must allow for the wind.

1509. Any mother can tell you a teen-ager's hangups don't include his clothes.

1510. There is nothing so powerful as truth—and often nothing so strange.

1511. The best insurance against an automobile accident is an afternoon nap.

1512. Most people look on budgeting as a nervous breakdown on paper!

1513. A young man was arrested while "necking" his girl on a freeway. He was charged with "driving while infatuated."

1514. TV soap operas do offer food for thought—if you like corn.

1515. It's very difficult for a person to stand on his own two feet when one foot is always in his mouth.

1516. You cannot whitewash yourself by darkening the reputation of others.

1517. Ideals may be beyond our reach but never beyond our fondest hopes.

1518. We are seldom able to see an opportunity until it has ceased to be one.

1519. Most people will fight much harder for special privileges than for equal rights.

1520. Everybody is now endowed with life, liberty and about $3,000 of national debt.

1521. When a man feels the world owes him a living, he is usually too lazy to collect it.

1522. What you don't know you can learn.

1523. A man's venom poisons himself more than its victim.

1524. Give some husbands enough rope and they will skip.

1525. It sure takes a fellow a long time to become an overnight success.

1526. Some people consider themselves friends because they have the same enemies.

1527. All our superhighways fall into one of two classes: over-crowded or under construction.

1528. Folks may have a right to say what they please, but most of them have more sense.

1529. Rock and Roll music may be just a passing fancy but it sure is making a lot of noise going through.

1530. Everybody wants to get what's coming to him—without getting what he deserves.

1531. There ought to be a better way to start the day than by getting up in the morning.

1532. Inflation is when you get money together to buy something, then find it isn't enough.

1533. It isn't a bad idea to keep still occasionally even when you know what you're talking about.

1534. Some of our speeding motorists might do well to remember that it is better to be a little late down here than too early up there.

1535. Early to bed and early to rise may be a sure sign that you're fed up with television.

1536. To a teen-ager, a VIP is a Very Ignorant Parent.

1537. One of the nicest things about Christmas is that you can make people forget the past with a present.

1538. The trouble with the average juvenile delinquent is not always apparent—sometimes it is two parents.

1539. What this country needs more than a change in the work week is a change in the WEAK work.

1540. People who don't believe in guardian angels haven't done much driving in rush-hour traffic.

1541. Faith gives us courage to face the present with confidence and the future with expectancy.

1542. Have you ever wondered what mothers find to talk about if their children aren't allergic to something?

1543. Some church members are like a tire with a slow leak—it takes a lot of pumping to keep them inflated.

1544. Why not go out on the limb—that's where the fruit is!

1545. A newlywed discussing married life, "So far all my wife can do is open cans and charge accounts."

1546. The most expensive things sometimes turn out to be those you get for nothing.

1547. Always work on the future. It is too late to ruin the past.

1548. Worry reminds us of a treadmill—it can wear you to a frazzle, and you still don't get anywhere.

1549. The most bored people are not the underprivileged but the overprivileged.

1550. A reputation once broken may possibly be repaired, but the world will always keep its eyes on the spot where the crack was.

1551. There are two types of people who say very little: The quiet folks and the gabby ones.

1552. Fishing is a laborious way of taking it easy.

1553. If life were as easy as we want it to be, most of us would sleep all the way through it.

1554. Imagination is what makes politicians think they're statesmen.

1555. Fifty years ago, minding one's children did not mean obeying them.

1556. Nothing causes so much matrimonial trouble as marriage.

1557. If you listen to the loan company commercial, you'll almost believe you can borrow yourself out of debt.

1558. It is far better to be a square than to be a lopsided smart aleck.

1559. The preacher who does not broaden and deepen his sermons ends up lengthening them.

1560. Arguing about your religion is much easier than practicing it.

1561. If you die tonight, would anybody be able to straighten out the mess you're in?

1562. United we stand; divided we pay alimony.

1563. Unless a man keeps a partition between his imagination and his facts, he is in danger of becoming just an ordinary liar.

1564. The haves and the have-nots are often the dids and did-nots.

1565. It is beginning to look like horse sense is becoming as scarce as horses.

1566. Teen-agers used to spin the bottle at parties. Now they give the pot a whirl.

1567. If college students are smart enough to run colleges and universities, they wouldn't be going to school.

1568. The President has the power to appoint and disappoint the members of his cabinet.

1569. Some recent laws would indicate the lawmakers not only passed the bar, but also stopped there.

1570. Too many Christian soldiers are now fraternizing with the enemy.

1571. Inflation has become so bad that it has hit the price of feathers. Even "down" is up.

1572. A neurotic builds castles in the air and a psychoanalyst collects the rent.

1573. What this country needs is a new kind of money that would be easier to save than spend.
1574. Keeping a budget is usually an orderly way of discovering you can't live on what you're making.
1575. A flea circus may be a good act, but it takes termites to bring down the house.
1576. Some folks can always find an excuse for putting off everything but a good time.
1577. Those who beef too much often land in the stew.
1578. One form of advertising that's a liability instead of an asset is a person's blowing his own horn.
1579. The average person brings most of his troubles on himself—and often uses poor judgment in choosing them.
1580. Said the girl graduate, "Four years of college! And WHOM has it got me?"
1581. Invest your money in taxes. They are bound to go up.
1582. The misleading thing about some preachers is that they carry their sermons around in a brief case.
1583. About the only thing free of charge these days is a rundown battery.
1584. A hypochondriac is one who wakes up every morning feeling like a million dollars—in pennies.
1585. The first concern of a politician is to be elected, the second, to be re-elected.
1586. A hobby is something you go mad over to keep from going crazy over other things.
1587. If the dollar bill shrinks any more, George Washington is going to have to get a haircut.
1588. To keep a teen-ager out of hot water—put dishes in it.
1589. Many people aim to do right but are just poor shots.
1590. The way to keep relatives from visiting you is to borrow money from the rich ones and lend money to the poor ones.
1591. Computers will never replace man entirely until they learn to laugh at the boss' jokes.
1592. A chemist whose name remains unknown says he has developed a new shaving lotion for men which is guaranteed to attract the ladies. It smells like a credit card.
1593. Promise yourself to worry less and pray more; to doubt less and trust more.
1594. Fame is a vapor, popularity an accident, riches take wings and only one thing endures—character.
1595. No one is more confusing than the fellow who gives good advice while setting a bad example.
1596. If you can't change facts, try bending your attitudes.
1597. Unless you can look interested when you are bored, you will never be a success socially.

1598. The perfect gift for a man who has everything would be a girl who knows what to do with it.

1599. It's only natural that student revolt should spread to high schools. After all, we wouldn't want our kids to enter college unprepared.

1600. The twenty-four billion dollars spent to put a man on the moon is the same amount spent by Americans on alcoholic beverages every year.

1601. The young people of today are no worse than we were; they just have more ways of making fools of themselves.

1602. Most things too good to be true, aren't.

1603. There's a new margarine on the market named RUMOR, because it spreads so quickly and easily.

1604. It takes two kinds of people to make the world—poets to write of the glories of autumn, and the rest of us to rake the leaves.

1605. The oldster who says he never felt better in his life can't even remember what it was like to feel good.

1606. Families that pray together, stay together—and families that work together—eat.

1607. The only people who aren't making good money these days are the counterfeiters.

1608. Maybe hard work won't kill a person, but who ever heard of a person resting himself to death?

1609. Temptations, unlike opportunities, will always give you a second chance.

1610. The law of supply and demand doesn't always hold true. Look how many reformers we have and how little reform!

1611. A hammer sometimes misses its mark—a bouquet never.

1612. The people who run our government evidently believe that the world is a big ball that revolves on its taxes.

1613. Sometimes it's the client's lawyer who should be punished for ignorance of the law.

1614. Father to son at college, "If you burn your draft card, I'll burn my checkbook."

1615. Some seem to think that the sins of omission are the ones they haven't gotten around to.

1616. Many a man saves everything but his soul.

1617. The question is not whether man descended from the monkey, but when he is going to stop descending.

1618. If everything seems to be going well, you have obviously overlooked something.

1619. Those who are sold on themselves still have to find a buyer's market.

1620. If this is a man's world it is because women don't want it.

1621. Rubbing elbows with a man will reveal things about him you never realized before. The same is true of rubbing fenders.

1622. In politics, we are still a two-party country—the appointed and the disappointed.

1623. You're not too old to learn—unless you are a teen-ager.

1624. Keep your temper to yourself, it's useless to others.

1625. Making a sin legal does not make it harmless.

1626. One smile in public is worth ten before the mirror.

1627. When the Roman Empire was falling apart, the people were kept busy with circuses. Now we have television.

1628. When you give somebody a piece of your mind, it's apt to be a pretty poor sample.

1629. The hand that rocks the cradle these days raids the refrigerator.

1630. People ought to be careful come election time because now and then an innocent man is sent to the legislature.

1631. The better a woman looks, the longer a man does.

1632. Don't expect to buy experience at a discount house.

1633. With many married couples, the sap seems to be running out of their tree of love.

1634. Most Americans have definite goals in life and attain them gradually—with the help of a finance company.

1635. Science had better not free the minds of men too much before it has tamed their instincts.

1636. Gossip is when someone gets wind of something and treats it like a cyclone.

1637. The measure of success is not whether you have a tough problem to deal with, but whether it's the same problem you had last year.

1638. Father to son entering college, "Remember, son, strange as it may seem to you, some of the professors will know more than you do."

1639. Disagreement is the lifeblood of democracy; dissention is its cancer.

1640. When the Lord gave us the Ten Commandments—He didn't mention amendments.

1641. Why is the virus that causes the common cold so hard to find, when it's so easy to catch?

1642. No one will ever know of your honesty and sincerity unless you give out some samples.

1643. The only thing a politician knows what to do with a tax is raise it.

1644. Parents these days scarcely bring up children; they finance them.

1645. The only man entitled to be asleep at the switch is the owner of an electric blanket.

1646. In this scientific age, the only impossible things are people.
1647. "Pull yourself together," is seldom said to anyone who can.
1648. A lot of today's troubles arise from workers who don't think, and from thinkers who don't work.
1649. The only state that permits a woman to work more than eight hours a day is matrimony.
1650. Don't mistake arrogance for wisdom; many people think they are wise when they are only windy.
1651. Those who are trying to live within their means may be lousing up the poverty program.
1652. If at first you don't succeed, hide your astonishment.
1653. Grass always looks greener on the other side of the fence— and on color TV.
1654. Some people insist upon always having the best of every-thing—except manners.
1655. The best time for parents is when the children are too old to cry and too young to borrow the car.
1656. A freeloader is a person who looks for a raft of friends to keep him aloat.
1657. Some politicians have been known to change their views rather radically. Some see the light, others feel heat.
1658. Space scientists have made an analysis of the lunar soil. It shows you that corn can't grow on the moon, but it's great for raising taxes.
1659. You can pick out an actor by the glazed look that comes into their eyes when the conversation wanders away from themselves.
1660. An intellectual person is so smart that he doesn't under-stand the obvious.
1661. The huge national debt our younger generation will inherit should keep them from one indulgence—ancestor worship.
1662. It takes only a little jack to lift a car, but a lot to keep it up.
1663. A baby is an angel whose wings decrease as his legs increase.
1664. Americans used to shout, "Give me liberty." Now they leave off the last word.
1665. Life is like a cafeteria. There are no waiters to bring success to you. You must help yourself.
1666. Every time history repeats itself the price goes up.
1667. Big men became big by doing what they didn't want to, when they didn't want to do it.
1668. A borrower is one who exchanges hot air for cold cash.
1669. Being afraid of what the neighbors might find out has prevented more devilment than most laws.
1670. Retirement is fine if you have two essentials: much to live on and much to live for.

71

1671. Watch your step. Everybody else does.
1672. A man who is immersed in business all week needs to come up for fresh air on Sunday.
1673. The man who never makes a mistake must get tired of doing nothing.
1674. Don't share your troubles; people are already over-supplied.
1675. Socialism is the paralysis that results from the free ride.
1676. A triangle is a square that didn't quite make it.
1677. Did you hear about the fellow who was so lazy his self-winding watch stopped?
1678. Many of us have friends who don't have ulcers, but everybody around them do.
1679. A hippie is social halitosis with hair on it.
1680. Summertime is playing, pleasure, parks, picnics, pools, paddling, perambulating, and then seeking a pawnbroker.
1681. All the dummies in the movies don't get thrown over cliffs.
1682. Government is a lot like your digestive system—if it works right, you hardly know you have it.
1683. Most of us jump into trouble—mouth first.
1684. The address of character is often carved on the corner of Adversity Avenue and Determination Drive.
1685. About the best way to do away with criminals is to stop raising them.
1686. A husband wanted to show his wife who was the boss so he bought her a mirror.
1687. No man would listen to you talk if he didn't know it was his turn next.
1688. If you have not taken a vacation by now you can at least figure what you've saved by listening to your friends who have just returned.
1689. A great opportunity will only make you look ridiculous unless you are prepared to meet it.
1690. No honest man is a successful fisherman.
1691. Some folks who think they are dreamers are just sleepers.
1692. A person who never makes a mistake gets pretty boring.
1693. Men love to praise integrity, but are slow to practice it.
1694. In prosperous times folks are better off than they are better.
1695. Please don't forget that one seventh of your time is spent on Mondays.
1696. Give a cat shelter, plenty of food, petting, and a feeling of security and she will stop catching mice. People are kinda like that.
1697. It is not the IQ but the I WILL which is important in education.
1698. Conversation is the art of telling people a little less than they want to know.

1699. An alcoholic is a person who lives in a DRAM world.
1700. Make friends; but remember that the best of friends will wear out if you use them too often.
1701. We really don't realize how wonderful today is until tomorrow.
1702. Love and a cough cannot be hid.
1703. People who take no chances generally have to take what is left over by those who do.
1704. The only time a politician can't demand a recount is when his wife gives birth to triplets.
1705. There's nothing wrong with some of the motion-picture market that a lot of non-attendance won't cure.
1706. The saddest sight along the way is a playboy who's too old to play!
1707. When your knees are knocking, it might help to kneel on them.
1708. A perfume clings to the hand that gives us roses.
1709. The trouble with law is lawyers.
1710. Some folks we know should take lessons in domestic silence.
1711. Tact will make you popular, provided you endure being taught many things that you already know.
1712. We'll never stop crime until we get over the idea we can hire or elect people to stop it.
1713. It is easier to follow the leader than to lead the followers.
1714. Some men do not know what their wives are worth until a judge sets the alimony payments.
1715. If you've given up on trying to get something open, tell a six-year-old not to touch it.
1716. The rhumba is a fox trot with the backfield in motion.
1717. Education is an ornament in prosperity and a refuge in adversity.
1718. It's a little difficult to reconcile the creed of some Christians with their greed.
1719. Remember the kindness of others; forget your own.
1720. When you say that you agree to a thing in principle you mean that you have not the slightest intention of carrying it out.
1721. Second-hand information is as unreliable as second-hand furniture. Both have been kicked around entirely too much.
1722. Medical doctors measure physical health by how the tongue looks. The Great Physician measures spiritual health by how the tongue acts.
1723. You can move an auto on gas, but not an audience.
1724. The reformer who says all scandals should be made public probably doesn't know the present price of print paper.

1725. It isn't WHAT the boys and girls know today that bothers their parents. It's HOW they found out.

1726. The Federal Government has no resources except the dollars it takes out of the pockets of the people.

1727. Progress is the development of more machines to provide more people with more leisure in which to be more bored.

1728. To stop the college professors from envying the janitors, their salaries are now being raised more than 30 percent.

1729. The best way to combat juvenile delinquency is to start at the bottom and work on it.

1730. You can tell when a man is well informed. His views are pretty much like your own.

1731. Politicians take the simple way out when they're in the dark—they simply cloud the issue.

1732. The lines actors like best are the ones in front of the box office.

1733. Changing our habits, like climbing a long flight of stairs, is something we do easier when we are young.

1734. Perhaps one of the reasons why we get so much free advice is that it's easier than helping.

1735. Philosophy is an inquiry into the wherefore of the therefore and the whyness of the which.

1736. It is very possible that flattery is something you hear about yourself that you wish were true.

1737. People once swapped gossip over the backyard fence. Now they do it in the laundromat.

1738. Our National Flower is the concrete cloverleaf.

1739. Give a politician a free hand and he'll put it in your pocket.

1740. Disillusionment is described as the reaction of a bridegroom who discovers that his beautiful wife looks that way, not by natural endowments, but only by courtesy of the cosmetic industry.

1741. As dangerous as ignorance is in the world, it is not as dangerous as knowledge without character.

1742. A fool is simply a person whose brand of folly differs from your own.

1743. It's peculiar how they've had to build expensive hospitals in almost every town since those old-fashioned grandmother remedies went out of style.

1744. What you don't know doesn't hurt—until you find out someone else is getting paid for knowing what you don't.

1745. A successful man is one who makes more money than his son at college can spend.

1746. The honeymoon is over when a husband doesn't notice his wife has something new until he gets the bill for it.

1747. A youth with his first cigar makes himself sick; a youth with his first girl makes other people sick.

1748. The best bridge between despair and hope is a good night's sleep.
1749. Nobody goes for that, "It's better to give than to receive," unless it's deductible.
1750. The greatest need of this generation is fewer automobile drivers and more wheelbarrow pushers.
1751. A husband wishes he had as much fun when he goes out as his wife thinks he does.
1752. Golf is a lot of walking, broken up by disappointment and bad arithmetic.
1753. The best thing a self-made man can do is deny it.
1754. Criminals seem to know their rights better than their wrongs.
1755. Inflation means that by the time a fellow gets a raise, it won't be enough.
1756. An old-timer can remember when parents and baby-sitters were the same people.
1757. College debts are obligations that with diligence, economy, and stern self-denial, father will be able to pay.
1758. Children need strength to lean on, a shoulder to cry on, and an example to learn from.
1759. He who has the habit of smiling at the cash register instead of the customer won't be smiling long.
1760. Faith without works is dead, which explains why so many are walking around in their own personal graveyard.
1761. A limousine is a car with a glass partition to shut out stupid remarks from the back seat.
1762. The Christian needs won't power as well as will power.
1763. Popular prices seem to be losing their popularity.
1764. When children get on the wrong track it is time to use the switch.
1765. It seems like our tax bodies have Robin Hood beat because he robbed only the rich.
1766. Brains and brakes prevent pains and aches.
1767. A good preacher scratches where members don't itch.
1768. The entrances to trouble are wide—the exits narrow.
1769. Learn to say kind things; nobody resents them.
1770. No amount of riches can atone for poverty of character.
1771. You can't understand all you read in the Bible, but you can obey what you do understand.
1772. The poor man is not he who is without a cent, but he who is without a dream.
1773. Constructive criticism is when I criticize you. Destructive criticism is when you criticized me.
1774. A job worth doing and friends worth having make life worth living.

1775. It's too bad that so many folks in passing out the milk of human kindness always skim it first.

1776. Some Christians are like neon lights—they keep going on and off.

1777. Twenty-five years ago most people thought that television was impossible—and lots of people still do.

1778. Every man needs a wife. Many things go wrong that can't be blamed on the government.

1779. In the old days, students went to college to get an education from the professors, but now it looks like some students think they ought to educate the professors.

1780. These are the days when the only thing that comes off on schedule is the button on your collar.

1781. It would be a far better world if we would all talk less and say more.

1782. Anger is of the greatest value when used sparingly.

1783. Men and nations do behave wisely, once all other alternatives have been exhausted.

1784. One reason it's so expensive to support the government is that so many people are holding it up.

1785. Not all sources of revenue have been tapped by the government. Pedestrians can still walk on a sidewalk without a license.

1786. A minister's prayer, "Lord, may the members of this church be as free with their money as they are with advice, and their minds as open as their mouths."

1787. The public will believe almost anything so long as it is not founded on truth.

1788. We defend our friends in the same proportion that we love them.

1789. Alimony is when two people find out they've made a mistake and one of them keeps on paying for it.

1790. The medical world has its problems. It's hard to give a man shock treatments once he's seen his wife in curlers.

1791. If thoughts could be read, faces might be redder.

1792. Americans have never before had more money and known less as to what becomes of it.

1793. The most valuable advice you can get usually comes from one who is most reluctant to give it.

1794. It is motive alone that gives character to the actions of men.

1795. One moment of folly can mean a lifetime of regret.

1796. Did you hear about the girl who was so slow-thinking she didn't even get to be a juvenile delinquent until she was 30?

1797. One of the most important things in life is to know how to keep problems from tackling you first.

1798. A man is never so weak as when some woman is telling him how strong he is.

1799. Many of those who embark upon the sea of matrimony know little about navigation.

1800. A new electronic device measures a millionth of an inch. It may be used for the next tax cut.